SELECTIVE FEEDING PROGRAMMES

OXFAM Practical Guide No. 1.

First published by Oxfam UK and Ireland in 1984

Reprinted in 1992, 1993, 1994, 1995, 2000, 2001, 2002, 2003

© Oxfam UK and Ireland 1984

ISBN 0 85598 097 4

A catalogue record for this publication is available from the British Library.

All rights reserved. Reproduction, copy, transmission, or translation of any part of this publication may be made only under the following conditions:

- with the prior written permission of the publisher; or
- with a licence from the Copyright Licensing Agency Ltd., 90 Tottenham Court Road, London W1P 9HE, UK, or from another national licensing agency; or
- for quotation in a review of the work; or
- under the terms set out below.

This publication is copyright, but may be reproduced by any method without fee for teaching purposes, but not for resale. Formal permission is required for all such uses, but normally will be granted immediately. For copying in any other circumstances, or for re-use in other publications, or for translation or adaptation, prior written permission must be obtained from the publisher, and a fee may be payable.

Available from:
Bournemouth English Book Centre, PO Box 1496, Parkstone, Dorset, BH12 3YD, UK
tel: +44 (0)1202 712933; fax: +44 (0)1202 712930; email: oxfam@bebc.co.uk

USA: Stylus Publishing LLC, PO Box 605, Herndon, VA 20172-0605, USA
tel: +1 (0)703 661 1581; fax: +1 (0)703 661 1547; email: styluspub@aol.com

For details of local agents and representatives in other countries, consult our website:
http://www.oxfam.org.uk/publications
or contact Oxfam Publishing, 274 Banbury Road, Oxford OX2 7DZ, UK
tel: +44 (0)1865 311 311; fax: +44 (0)1865 312 600; email: publish@oxfam.org.uk

Our website contains a fully searchable database of all our titles, and facilities for secure on-line ordering.

Published by Oxfam GB, 274 Banbury Road, Oxford OX2 7DZ, UK.

Oxfam GB is a registered charity, no. 202 918, and is a member of Oxfam International.

SELECTIVE FEEDING PROGRAMMES

Oxfam Practical Guide No 1

INDEX

Introduction

Part One: Assessments and Surveys
Chapter 1 Malnutrition: definitions and descriptions
Chapter 2 Anthropometric measurements
Chapter 3 Assessment and information gathering
Chapter 4 Surveys and interpreting and using results

Part Two: Selective Feeding Programmes
Chapter 5 Feeding Programmes
Chapter 6 Supplementary Feeding Programmes
Chapter 7 Therapeutic Feeding Programmes
Chapter 8 Health care and Vitamin deficiencies
Chapter 9 Training of Community Health Workers in nutrition
Chapter 10 Reporting/Monitoring and Evaluation of Programmes

Part Three: Appendices
1. Checklist
2. Weight/height tables
3. Contents of Oxfam Feeding Kits and other resources
4. Standard food tables and nutritional requirements
5. Recipes
6. Directions for construction of length board, height stick and height arch for measuring children
7. Further reading

Background

This Practical Guide is based on 'Selective Feeding Procedures', which was originally written by Sue Peel as a technical manual to accompany the Oxfam Feeding Kits (Supplementary and Therapeutic). The Kits were based on the needs experienced during relief work in the Wollo and Ogaden famines in Ethiopia during 1973-75.

This revision aims to incorporate what we have learnt since that time. The scope has been widened to include assessment and nutrition surveys and the Feeding Kits have also been modified.

INTRODUCTION

An initial assessment of health and nutritional needs is essential in determining an appropriate response within the refugee community.

Where people are completely dependent on outside food sources, the priority should always be to ensure an adequate general ration of appropriate foods in order to maintain health and nutrition status.

However, if the current situation has been preceded by a long period of drought or displacement, a significant number of people are likely to be malnourished on arrival at the relief centre, and in need of nutritional rehabilitation.

An objective nutrition survey will help to indicate

    (a) if there is a need for Selective Feeding Programmes, and
    (b) whether or not such Programmes should have priority.

Any decision to implement these Programmes should be a joint one with the refugee communities themselves. Right from the start they should be involved in the planning, organisation and management of the Programmes, ensuring that the response is appropriate, acceptable, and at a level that the community is able to support.

Selective Feeding Programmes should not continue as long-term interventions unless there is a clearly indicated *nutritional* need.

Continuous monitoring and repeat nutrition surveys will enable modifications to be made to meet changing needs and in planning the closure of Supplementary and Therapeutic Centres.

Before considering in more detail possible solutions to technical problems, it is important to look closely at the community of refugees or displaced people. Family, social and economic structures will exist which will affect the outcome of any relief programme. The refugees or displaced people are often most able to help themselves and are, to a great extent, able to take responsibility for their own welfare.

Ill-considered assistance can create a needless dependency. Inputs must be in the form of a sensitive response to needs that the refugees and local organisations are unable to meet on their own.

PART ONE: ASSESSMENTS AND SURVEYS

CHAPTER 1.

MALNUTRITION: DEFINITIONS AND DESCRIPTIONS
Malnutrition can be divided into two broad groups:
1.1. Protein Energy Malnutrition
1.2. Vitamin and mineral deficiencies

1.1. Protein Energy Malnutrition (PEM)
This can be the most important health problem at times of nutritional emergencies, and can present in various forms.

1.1.1. Marasmus
This results from insufficient food (i.e. not enough calories).

In its early stages marasmus is recognised only as loss of weight. As the disease progresses severe wasting occurs until the skin hangs loosely from the bones, especially around the buttocks where the lack of fat and muscle causes the skin to hang like 'baggy pants'. The eyes become sunken, producing an 'old man's face'.

Marasmus can be confused with dehydration; very often children suffer from both. Dehydrated children appear more sick, have a rapid pulse and usually a fever, and the skin of the abdomen is particularly inelastic. When conscious, children are usually very thirsty.

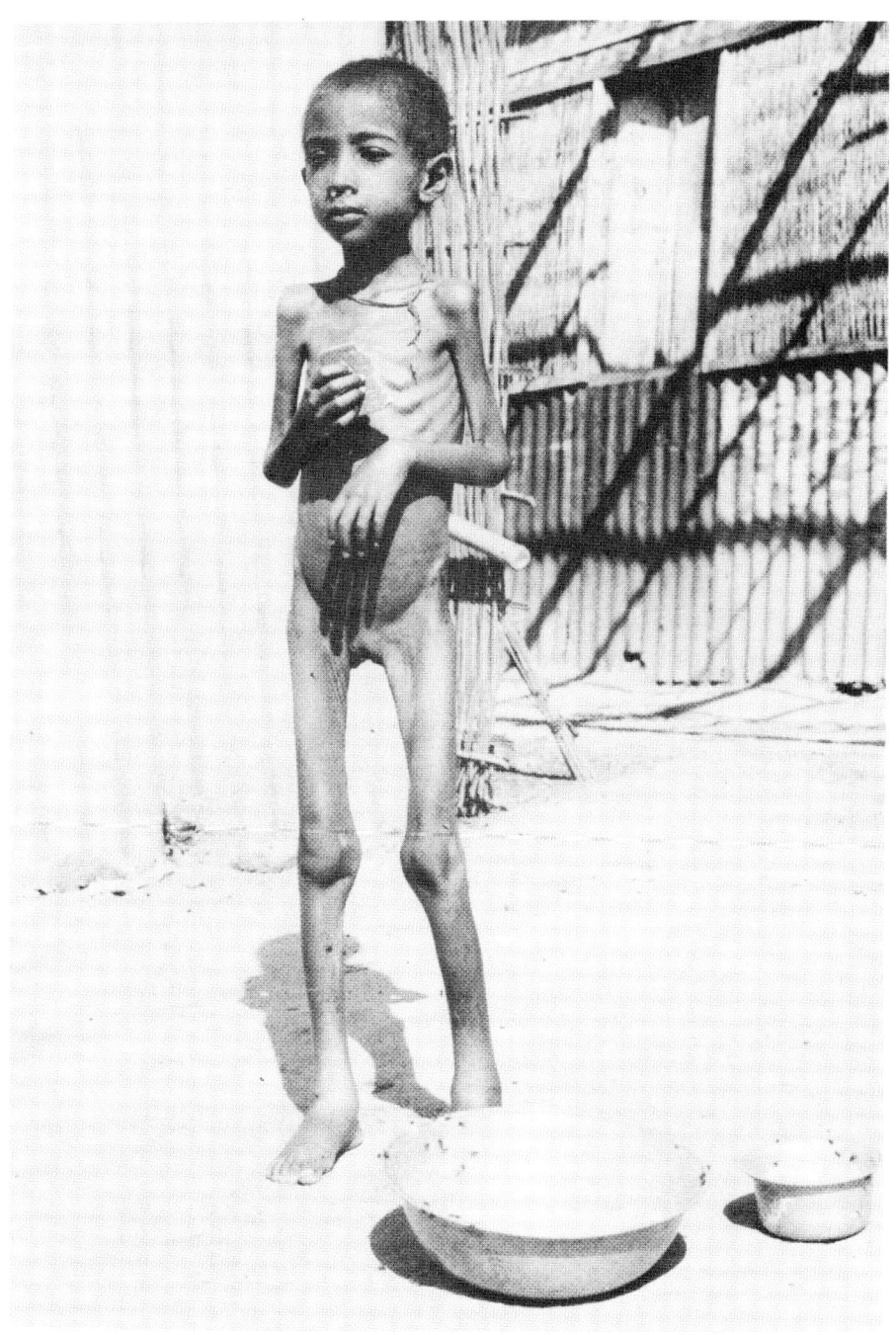

Marasmic child

1.1.2. Kwashiorkor

Under 'normal' conditions kwashiorkor is most frequently found in children recently displaced from the mother's breast by the arrival of a new baby, or following acute infections. In famine conditions it can affect any age group, although it is usually still seen mainly in young children. *Swelling* or *oedema* is the earliest and most important sign of kwashiorkor, the swelling usually starting in the feet and lower legs although it can occur all over the body. To check for oedema, press the area on the back of the foot or shin and see if a pit remains when the finger is removed (pitting oedema). Sometimes the child has a swollen face - called a 'moon face' - and ascites (swollen abdomen). The hair often becomes light in colour, brittle, and may pull out easily.

As the child's condition deteriorates, other changes will occur: the skin may flake off, leaving raw, weeping areas. The child becomes miserable and irritable, and finally shows total lack of interest and apathy prior to death.

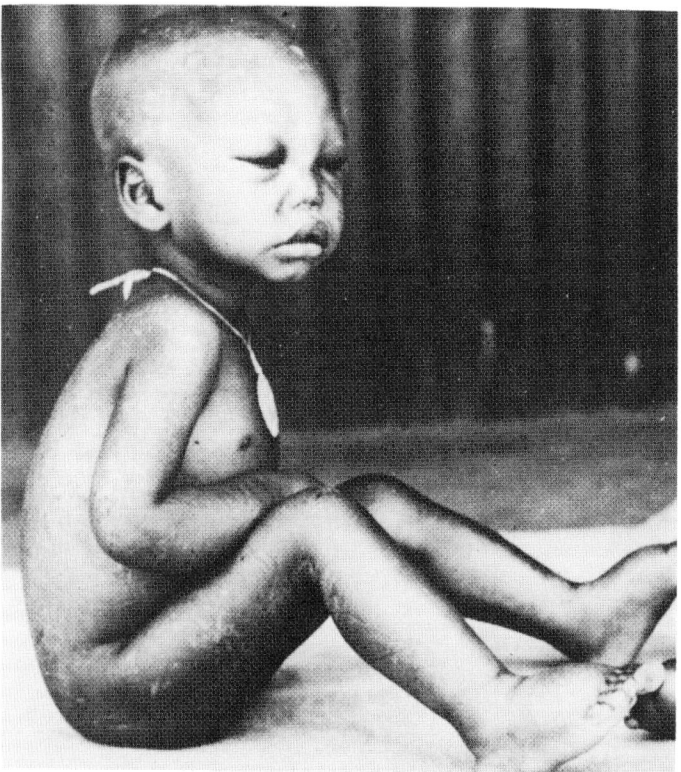

1.1.3. Marasmic-kwashiorkor:
is a common combination of the above two conditions. The child appears thin and wasted, with swollen lower limbs.

1.2. Vitamin and mineral deficiency

1.2.1. Anaemia

Anaemia is a low level of haemoglobin in the blood. The main causes are parasitic infections (particularly hookworm and malaria), and low intake or poor absorption of iron and folic acid. Malnourished people are often severely anaemic; this can be recognised by looking at the tongue, finger nails, or the inside of the lower eyelid, which appear exceptionally pale. The presence of anaemia is usually measured subjectively but (frequently) inaccurately; more accurate measurements of anaemia levels normally require access to simple laboratory facilities.

1.2.2. Vitamin A deficiency (Xerophthalmia or nutritional blindness)

This is the most important vitamin deficiency. It can lead to permanent blindness if not recognised and treated.

Most Vitamin A comes from vegetable sources (green vegetables, yellow fruits and vegetables). A sudden reduction in the diet does not immediately produce a rise in the incidence of cases, since Vitamin A is stored in the liver. There may be a delay of several months before signs of deficiency show.

Warning signs and symptoms

i. Night Blindness: those affected are unable to see in poor light, i.e. after sunset, inside huts, etc., while those with normal sight are still able to see well. Mothers may recognise that the night vision of their child is poor.

ii. Areas on the conjunctiva become dry and dull (xerosis).

iii. Collection of foamy material on the conjunctiva (Bitot's spots) usually on the outer side of the iris, and often triangular in shape.

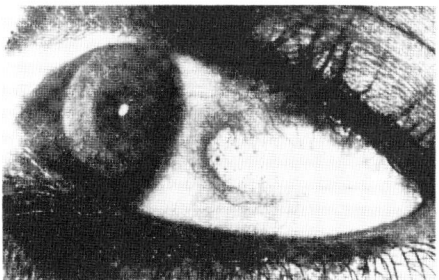

iv. The most severe signs are clouding, ulceration and (even within the space of a few hours) perforation of the cornea leading to loss of eye content and eventual blindness.

The presence of any of these warning signs in even a few children can indicate that many more may be at risk and should be investigated.

1.2.3. Vitamin B1 deficiency (Beriberi)

This occurs in areas where the people have had to exist on a starchy staple food e.g. cassava, white polished rice, and can become a problem when refugees are given *only* polished rice during the course of a relief action, e.g. Thai/Khmer experience.

Several forms exist:

i. Moderate deficiency: signs or symptoms include loss of appetite, malaise and weakness, especially in the legs. This may last for several months.

ii. 'Dry Beriberi' - can lead to paralysis of the limbs.

iii. 'Wet Beriberi' with swelling of the body (oedema) and heart failure which can lead to sudden death.

An average daily intake of 1mg thiamine will prevent beriberi; sources include undermilled cereals, some vegetables and green leaves.

1.2.4. Vitamin B deficiency (Pellagra)

This deficiency is seen mainly amongst people who use a predominantly maize and sorghum diet. It is characterised by a skin rash on those parts of the body exposed to sunlight.

1.2.5. Vitamin C deficiency (Scurvy)

In long-term disaster situations, scurvy can occur when the basic general ration contains inadequate Vitamin C, i.e. less than 10 mg/day.

It is recognised by swollen, bleeding gums, or swollen, painful joints; but it can be confused with other illnesses.

Sources of Vitamin C include fresh fruits (especially oranges, lemons, limes etc.) and vegetables.

1.2.6. Specific deficiencies may need to be treated at two levels:

i. Individual level

ii. Public Health (mass) approach.

The best way of preventing such deficiencies is through an adequate diet. The distribution of multivitamin tablets is usually a waste of time and money as most of them contain only very small quantities of individual vitamins, and may create a false sense of security.

For details of individual treatments and approaches, please see Chapter 8.

CHAPTER 2.

ANTHROPOMETRIC MEASUREMENTS AND SCREENING

There are two main ways of assessing malnutrition in emergencies:

2.1. Weight in relation to height

2.2. Arm circumference

For the longer-term development phase the following methods are also used:

2.3. Weight for age

2.4. Height for age

2.1. Weight for height

It is possible to assess the severity of PEM by comparing the weight of a malnourished child with the weight of a well-nourished child of the same height. This is the best method of assessment of acute malnutrition, provided there is no oedema present. A normal, well-nourished child of a certain height can be expected to be of a certain weight. A series of these 'normals' has been calculated and they are considered to be 100% or standard weight for height. For example:

wt/ht over 100% = overweight

wt/ht 80 - 100% = adequately nourished

wt/ht 70 - 80% = moderately malnourished

wt/ht 70% and/or oedema = severely malnourished

Any child with oedema should be considered malnourished, regardless of weight.

This percentage weight for height is calculated as follows:

$$\frac{\text{Actual weight of a child} \times 100}{\text{Normal weight of a child of the same height.}} = \% \text{ of standard weight/height.}$$

Thus if a child weighed say 12kg and the normal weight for a child of his height was 15kg, then that child would be $\frac{12 \times 100}{15} = 80\%$ weight for height.

Weight for height tables are available (Appendix 2) to make this calculation a quick and easy procedure.

In surveys the weight of each child can be plotted on a weight for height graph which will indicate the state of nutrition of the community.

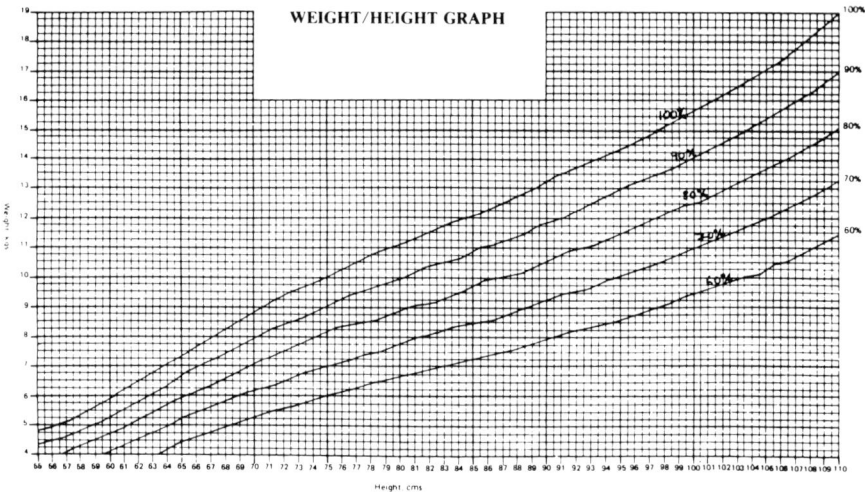

How to measure

Accurate weighing for each child is essential if a true assessment of nutritional status and subsequent progress is to be made. The portable hanging scales are strong and reliable and can be hung from a tree or a hook in the ceiling, but care must be taken not to suspend them too high, to avoid fear. The scales must be attached securely and allowed to hang free. The needle must be adjusted to zero with the sling or basket attached before each child is weighed. The child is then placed in the sling or basket hanging from the scales. Older children can hold onto the hook themselves.

NOTE: these scales should be checked with a standard weight at the beginning of each session and changed as necessary. Always have a spare set available.

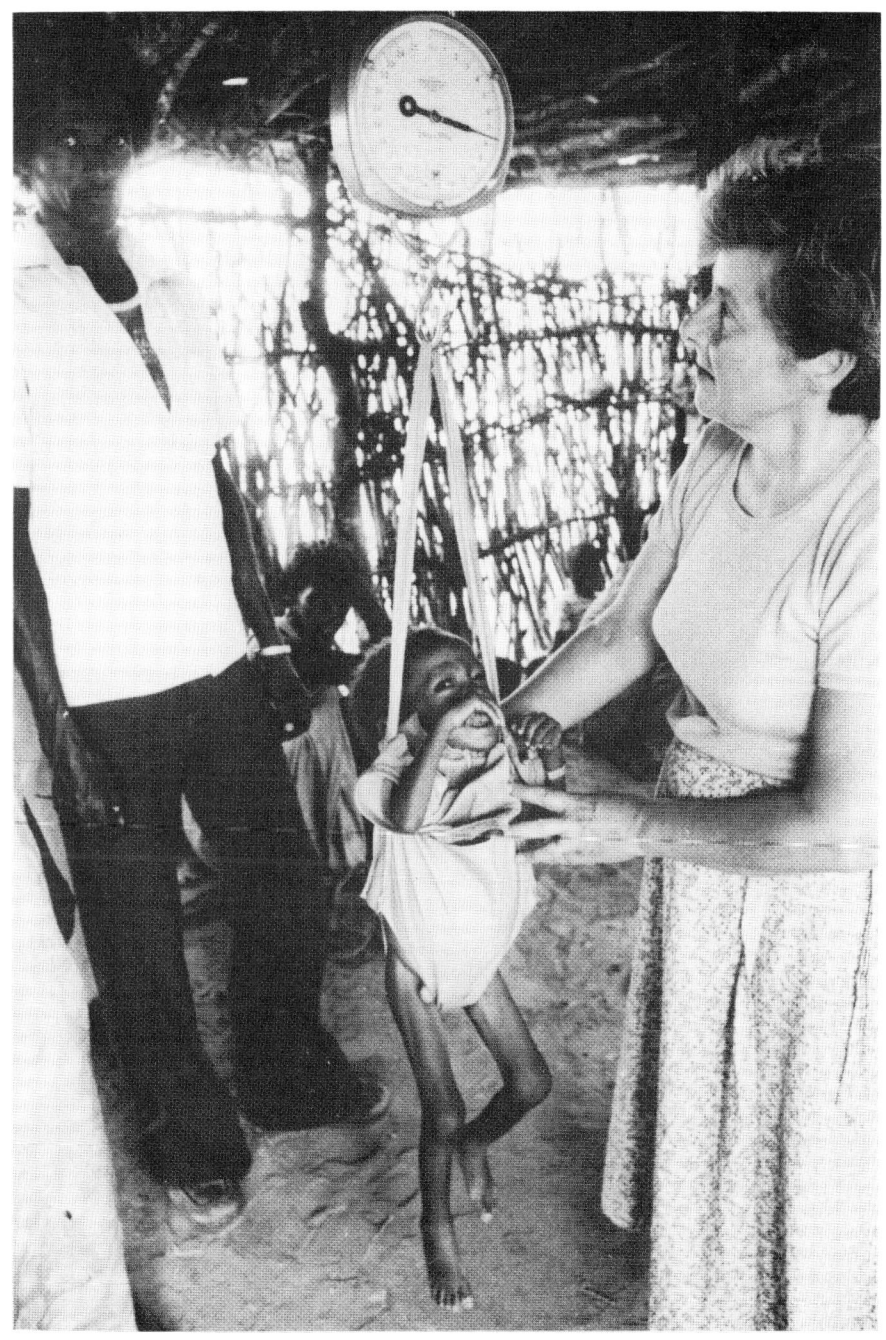
Weighing a child on the portable hanging scales

Heights and lengths: if a child is able to stand, her/his height may be measured using a graduated height stick. All children below 2 years old (85cm) should have their length measured; also those too weak to stand.

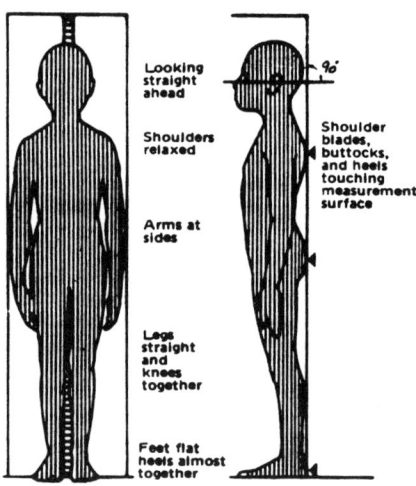

The child must stand up straight, back to the scale, heels together, looking straight ahead. The height can then be read off the scale and recorded accurately.

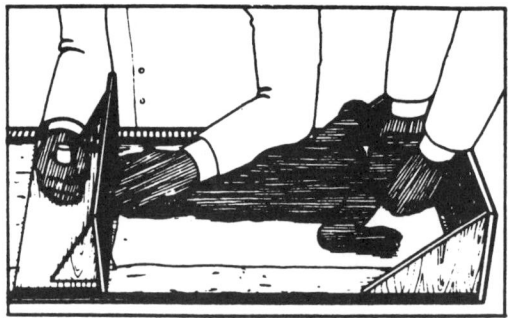

The child is laid on the board with his head against the fixed base. A movable end is adjusted to rest lightly against the child's feet. Holding this firmly in place, the length of the child can be read off a scale running along the edge of the board. Height sticks and length boards can easily be made locally (see Appendix 6).

Weight for height charts (SCF charts)

A tri-coloured chart has been developed to assist in the assessment of malnutrition. Children are first weighed, and then placed standing in front of their weight column. The colour immediately behind the top of their head indicates nutritional status:

Upper red = 60-69%
Lower red = 70-79%
Yellow   = 80-89%
Green   = 90% and over

These charts are easy to use as they cut out the need for percentage tables. There may however be some initial confusion as a thin child appears higher on the chart than the level of a well-fed child (too thin for her/his height), whereas on a Road to Health chart, a thin child appears *below* the level of a well-fed child. Weight for height charts have their own recording cards.

Advantages of weight for height (length)

i. it is not necessary to know the child's age
ii. the weight is related to stature so that a short, plump child which might be underweight *for its age* is not registered as malnourished, i.e. weight for height allows for stunting and shows up acute malnutrition or thinness
iii. the weight is a useful measure for following up the individual child as well as for evaluating the overall progress of Feeding Programmes

The disadvantages of weight for height (length)

i.   it can be time-consuming
ii. it requires two measurements which can lead to a risk of errors
iii. it requires the ability to read tables and keep records
iv. occasionally misleading results can be obtained: oedema, swollen abdomen (ascites), heavy worm loads, etc., can affect the weight, making the child appear heavier and therefore less malnourished. Measuring should be accompanied by a rapid clinical assessment, looking for a few common signs: 'baggy pants', oedema, poor muscle tone, swollen abdomen, etc.

Practical problems

Both measurements must be accurate. The field worker should be aware of some factors affecting accuracy; for instance, when measuring heights, dirt floors can rapidly become compressed or worn away, so that children appear shorter as the day goes on. A way around this is to stand the child on a thin, flat piece of wood and adjust the scale accordingly.

Accuracy in recording results is also essential and it is worth while to double check every twentieth recording, for example.

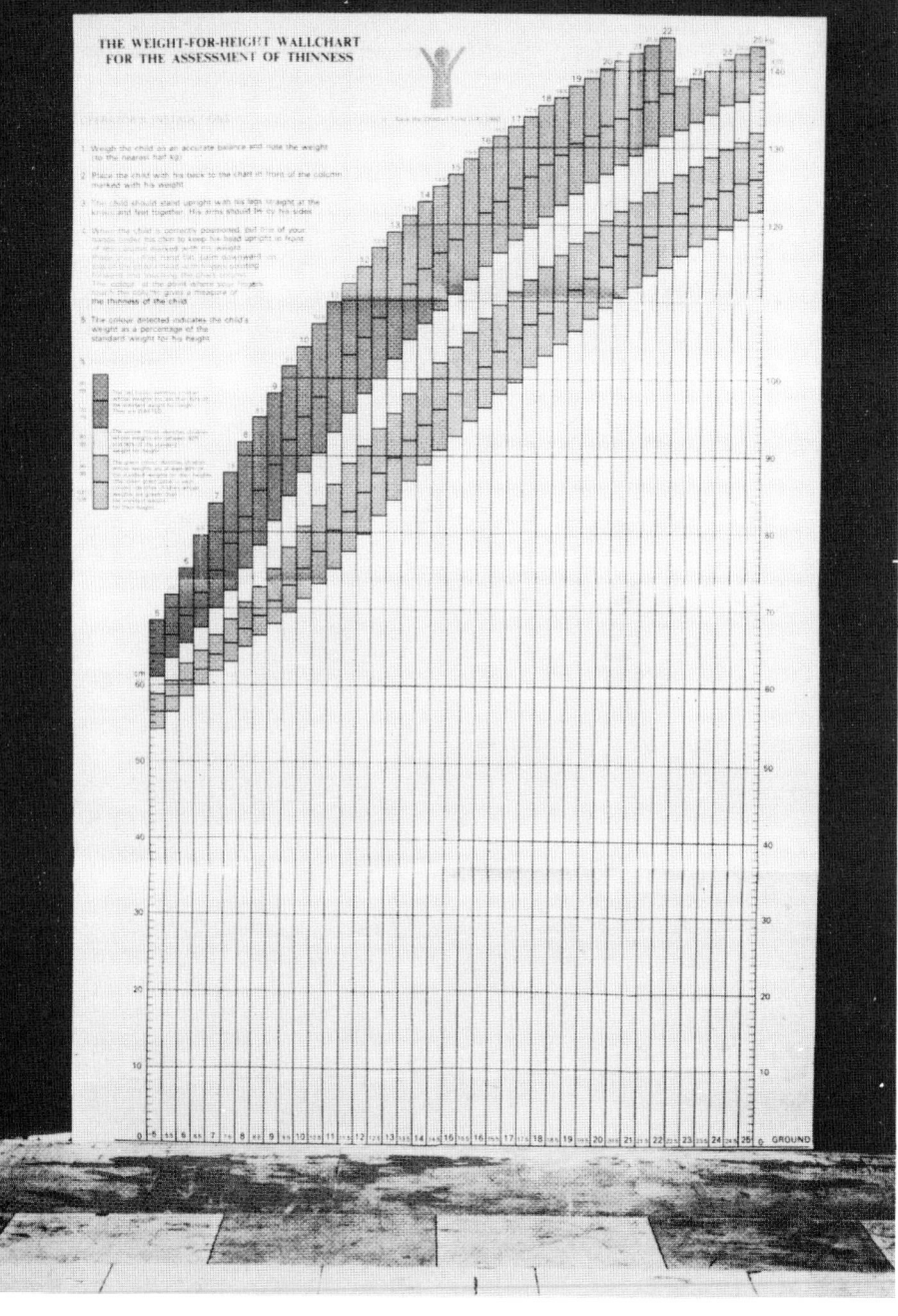

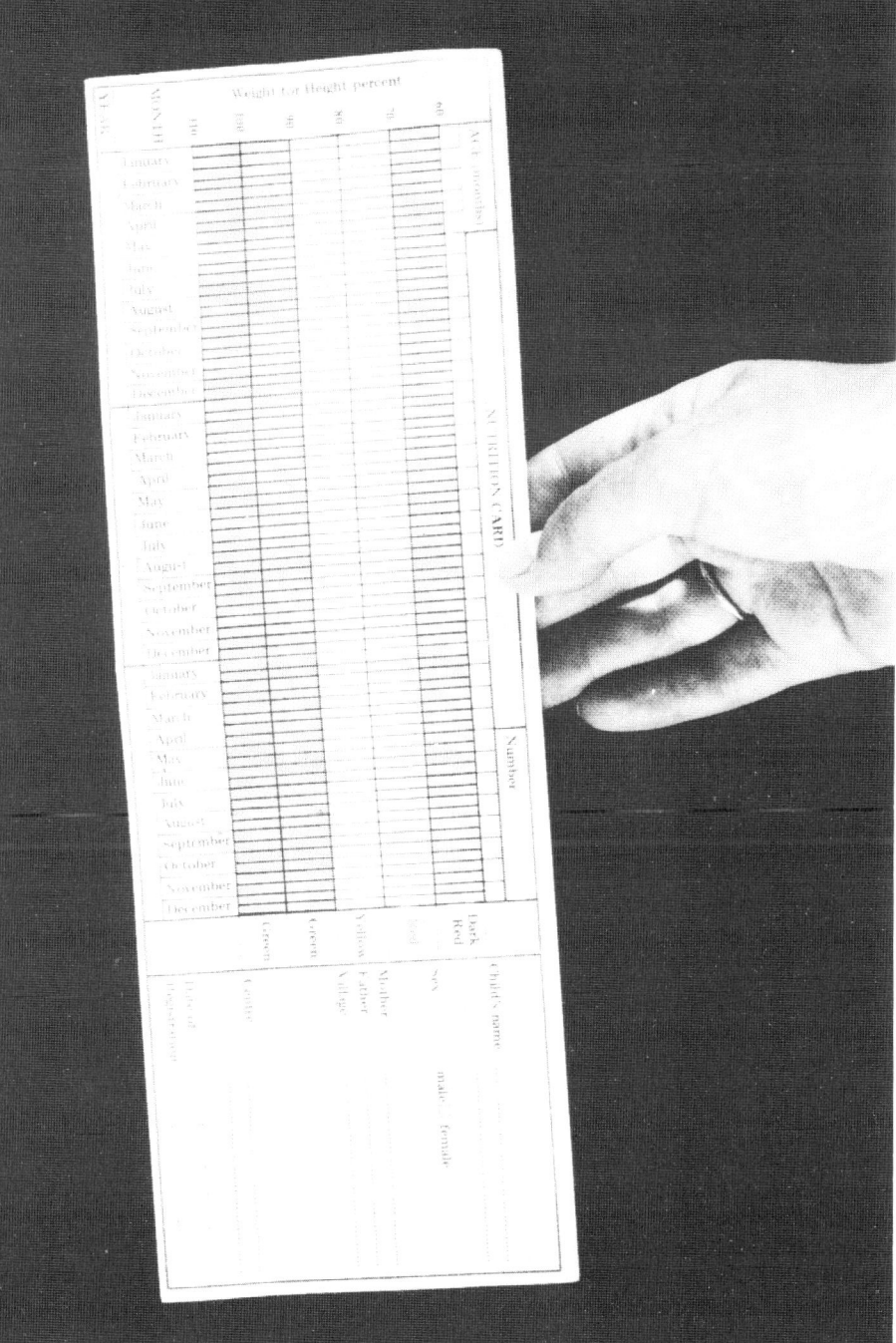

2.2. Arm circumference

It is possible to assess the nutritional status of a child using the measurement of the mid-upper arm circumference (MUAC). The advantage of this method is that the normal arm circumference of children between the ages of 1 and 5 years remains relatively static, so that standard cut-off points can be used. It is not essential to know the exact age; a normal 1 year old has six or more teeth and can stand or walk; a 5 year old is normally less than 115cm tall.

Method

The left arm of the child should hang in a relaxed position. The arm circumference is measured mid-way between the elbow and the shoulder. The tape should be wrapped closely around the arm but must not be twisted or pulled tight.

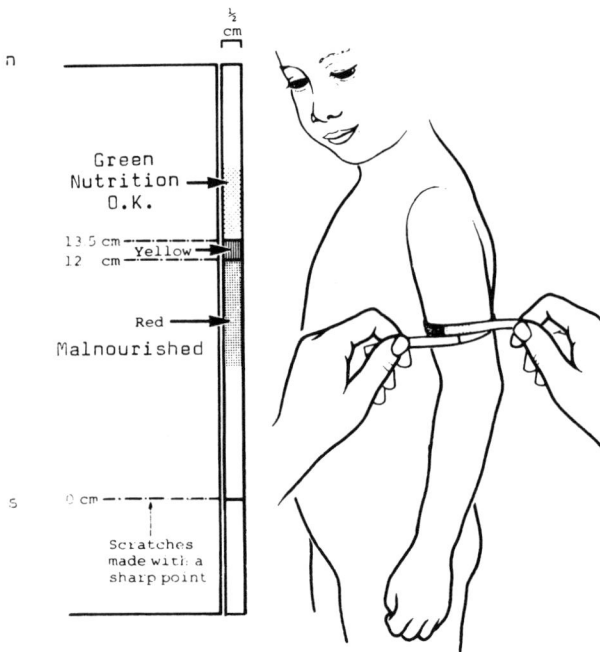

It is helpful to put a mark at the 10cm line and read off the measurement from that point. If this is 19.5cm then the arm circumference is 9.5cm. The following classification should be used until further research has been done:

MUAC over 13.5cm = adequately nourished
MUAC 12 to 13.5cm = moderately malnourished
MUAC below 12cm and/or oedema = severely malnourished

2.3 Weight for age

In the initial stages of a disaster, weight for age is not as useful for assessment as weight for height, because:

i. it is often difficult to assess age accurately. People rarely have accurate birth dates, but local knowledge can help, such as "he was born during the last rains"

ii. the plump stunted child may be recorded malnourished on the Road to Health chart, i.e. a low weight for age does not necessarily mean that the child is thin

iii. it always paints a more pessimistic picture than weight/height

However, once the camp becomes established, patient-retained Road to Health charts become very useful to measure progress of children.

Once the weight and age of the child are discovered, this can then be recorded either as a percentage of normal or it can be plotted on a weight for age (Road to Health) chart.

See charts on Pp. 16 & 17.

2.4. Height for age

This measures chronic malnutrition and long-term stunting and is not useful in planning Feeding Programmes in emergency situations.

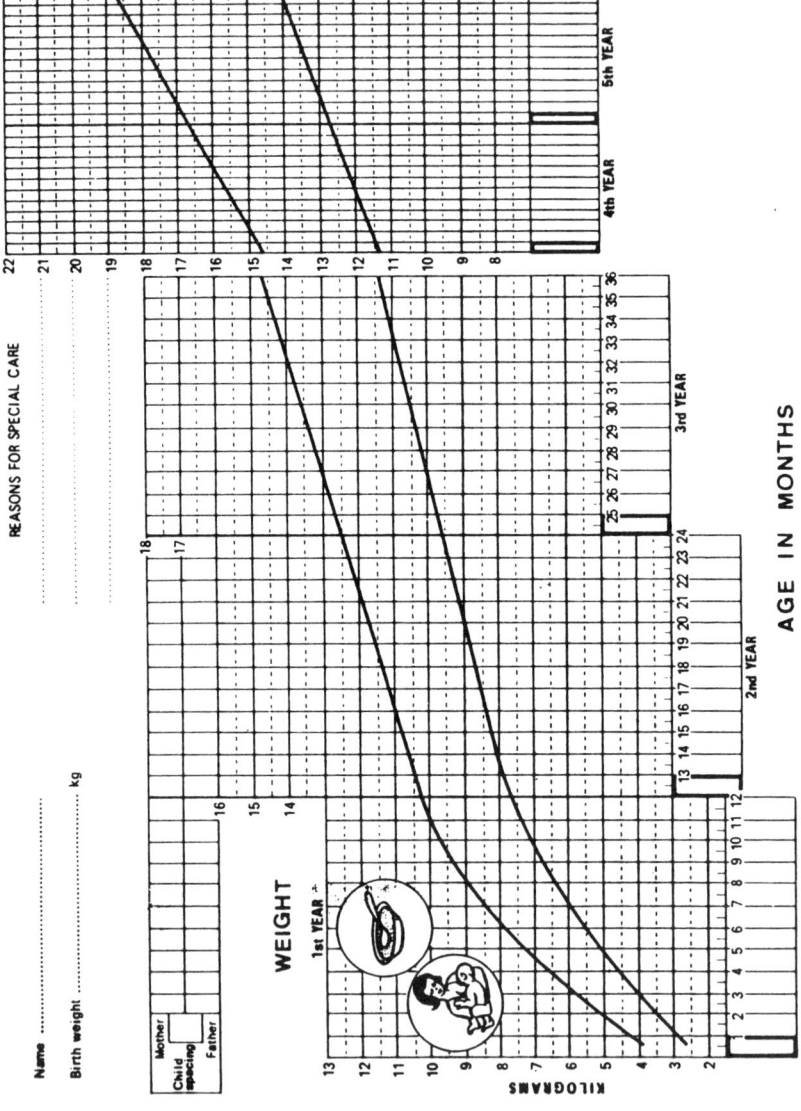

THE BACK OF A ROAD TO HEALTH CHART FOR THE COLLECTION OF INFORMATION ON THE CHILD AND THE FAMILY

GROWTH CHART

Health centre	Child's No.
Child's name	
Date first seen	Birthday
Mother's name	Registration No.
Father's name	Registration No.
Where the family lives (address)	

BROTHERS AND SISTERS

Year/birth	Boy/Girl	Remarks	Year/birth	Boy/Girl	Remarks

IMMUNIZATIONS

ANTI-TUBERCULOSIS (BCG)
Date of immunization ___

SMALLPOX
Date of immunization ___
Date of scar inspection ___
Date of reimmunization ___

WHOOPING COUGH, TETANUS AND DIPHTHERIA
Date of first injection ___
Date of second injection ___
Date of third injection ___

POLIOMYELITIS
Date of first immunization ___
Date of second immunization ___
Date of third immunization ___

MEASLES
Date of immunization ___

APPOINTMENTS

CHAPTER 3.

ASSESSMENT AND INFORMATION-GATHERING

Good food, an adequate water supply, shelter and sanitation are the most important physical needs of refugee and displaced communities.

3.1. General assessment

It is important that, when assessing the situation, relief workers look at factors which affect the nutritional status of the population, for example: water supply and sanitation, communicable diseases, overcrowding, and general environmental health.

A general assessment of the camp can be made under the following headings:

i. demography and background
ii. food
iii. water
iv. sanitation
v. shelter
vi. logistics
vii. health care
viii. rehabilitation

A checklist relating to each of these can be found in Appendix 1. This should be used as an aide memoire rather than a questionnaire.

3.2. Camp population

It is essential to have some idea of the total camp population and of how this total figure is made up (i.e. how many men, women and children). Ideally a census should be carried out, which can be used to indicate numbers in high risk groups and assist with programme planning. (See Checklist in Appendix 1.)

However, for political reasons authorities may be reluctant to make known the size of the camp population.

3.3. Nutritional information

It is especially important to understand the normal cooking and eating habits of the people (e.g. often eggs and some meat are forbidden to lactating and pregnant women). Other important, though not directly relevant, subjects are traditions related to social structures and religion. Time spent in understanding people helps to generate the trust and co-operation which are essential in overcoming many practical problems.

Surveys give some idea of the present situation and what has happened in the past. The nutritional status of the camp in the days and months to come will clearly depend on general food availability and health measures. It is therefore important to learn as much as possible about what the community is eating and how it gets its food. Particular attention should be paid to vulnerable groups. The most important questions are:

3.3.1. History

A brief recent history of period of displacement, drought or famine prior to arrival at the relief centre. Duration of stay in relief centre is also important (there may be considerable variation between 'settled' people and 'new arrivals').

3.3.2. What types of food are people eating?

This may be a combination of relief foods (maize, wheat, oil, sugar, and milk derivatives in various combinations) and local produce. Occasionally there are small markets where some relief goods are exchanged for local relishes to which the refugees are accustomed and like. It is useful to know if young children are normally fed differently from adults, and attention should also be paid to the acceptability of relief foods.

3.3.3. How much food are people getting? Is distribution fair?

It may be useful to survey a few family households from different sections of the relief centre. This could give an idea of average family/daily intake. (See Chapter 5 for general ration requirements.)

3.3.4. How is the food distributed and cooked?

It is useful to know how often food supplies are handed out and to whom. How does the food reach individual families and how is it shared within the family?

After a while fuel for cooking almost invariably becomes a severe problem, and it will be useful to know how refugees are handling this problem.

3.3.5. How, if at all, are the 'at risk' groups helped?

Are they given extra rations - if so, what? Is the food eaten at a Feeding Centre or in the home? Do people understand that the extra rations are a *supplement* to the general diet and not a substitute for normal food?

3.3.6. Health facilities

What facilities already exist in the Centre? How well are they coping? How well staffed? Are they assisting the malnourished in the community?

3.3.7. Water supply

The nutritional status of communities is greatly influenced by the availability of sufficient *quantities* of reasonably *good quality* water. If water is inadequate the personal hygiene and food preparation will suffer. The diarrhoea and infections which follow will undermine any good effects of food.

It is important to look at the source of the water, how it is collected and distributed, and how stored in the home. In addition, a very rough estimate of consumption per person should be made. Anything less than 15 litres per head should indicate the need for immediate action, as should a recent history of a diarrhoeal disease epidemic, or high incidence of eye or skin infections, e.g. trachoma and scabies. (See 'Oxfam's Practical Guide to Refugee Health Care', Appendix 6.)

CHAPTER 4.

SURVEYS AND INTERPRETING AND USING RESULTS

Before any surveys (pilot or general) are undertaken, the co-operation and agreement of community leaders should be obtained and the community itself involved.

4.1. Surveys

It is essential that a nutrition survey is done in the initial assessment to determine the severity of the situation and the need (if any) for action.

Nutritional assessment should include two aspects:

i. measuring the nutritional status of a sample of the children 1-5 years old. This gives an idea of what has happened in the past and the amount and degree of existing malnutrition.

ii. looking at the effectiveness of current food availability and/or Feeding Programme in relation to needs and normal diet of the population. This helps in planning food supplies and anticipating future problems. (See Chapter 3.)

4.2. Assessing nutritional status of the population

Objective surveys provide a baseline against which future surveys can be compared when measuring the effectiveness of what has been done and deciding whether the situation is improving or deteriorating, so that interventions can be adjusted to suit changing needs.

The Oxfam Mini Survey Kit is useful where equipment for carrying out a survey or screening cannot be found locally. (See Appendix 3.)

4.3. Selecting whom and where to survey

In times of food scarcity, the first group to show signs of malnutrition are the young children; for this reason, a random sample of children (1-5 years) can be used as an indicator of the nutritional status of the community.

It is not necessary to measure *all* the children, but in any location a minimum of 200 should be measured (100 females and 100 males). If there are fewer children than this at a location, they should all be measured. In camps of populations over 10,000, at least 400 children should be measured.

A nutrition survey must measure a representative sample of all the children (1-5 years) in the camp. Often surveys only measure those thinner children who may already be included in a Feeding Programme; this will not give a true picture of the general situation. To achieve this, it is necessary to use a sampling method.

4.4. Sampling

The following methods can be used:

4.4.1. Sequential

In relief centres with organized rows of huts, houses or tents, visit every tenth house and measure all the children under 5 years old in that house; *any child who is away from home should be brought back and measured.*

If one area of the relief centre is new or different, it should be surveyed separately. It may be helpful to draw a rough plan or map of the different sections or areas of the camp.

4.4.2. Clustering

If the layout is unplanned, cluster sampling can be done. Using a rough map, divide the camp into eight equal areas; go to the centre of one area, choose a direction by spinning a stick and walk in a straight line counting the number of huts passed; then choose at random a number between one and the total number of huts passed in that section; if the number is six, go to the sixth hut in line from the starting point and measure *all* the children under 5 years old in that hut. Go to the nearest hut and repeat, and continue until at least 30 children have been measured.

Repeat the process in each of the eight areas of the camp.

(For further details on random surveys see 'The Management of Nutritional Emergencies in Large Populations' - WHO, Geneva.)

There are many variations on the methods described here and relief workers should not be bound to any one system. It is, however important to understand the principle of sampling: a nutrition survey *must* measure a sample of *all* the children.

4.5. Who should do the survey

Ideally, responsible trained members of the refugee community should be involved in carrying out the survey under guidance. In order to iron out unforeseen problems it is essential to carry out a small *pilot survey*, say on five dwellings. Technique and results can then be checked.

Each survey team will need:

    a height stick and length board

    scales

    tape measure

    record book or pad or prepared survey sheet

    pens or pencils

4.6. The survey

Ideally in each dwelling the weight and height of all children under 5 years or 115cm in height are recorded, as well as the prevalence of oedema.

However, where time and experience are limited it will suffice to record the arm circumference of each child between the ages of 1 and 5 years, and the presence or absence of oedema.

Obviously, more information (e.g. about predominant symptoms and disease) can be gathered, but it is best initially to keep the enquiry simple and short. It may be useful, though, to keep a simple tally of, for instance, eye problems, scabies, etc.

Information can be recorded in a variety of ways:

Table 1: Weight/height

No.	Wt	Ht	%	Oedema	Male	Female
1.	7.5kg	79cm	70%	+		
2.	18.8kg	110cm	100%	−		
3.						

Table 2: Arm circumference

Over 13.5cm	13.5 - 12cm	Under 12cm	Oedema	Male	Female
卌	III	卌	II		

Table 3

Extra columns could be included showing, for instance:

Eye signs	Scabies	Anaemia			

4.7. Presentation of results

Once all information has been recorded, the number of children in each category is totalled and the percentages calculated, for example:

Table 4

	WT/HT over 80%	WT/HT 70-80%	WT/HT under 70%	Total children
children	170	22	8	200
percentage	85%	11%	4%	

Table 5

	MUAC over 13.5cm	MUAC 13.5 - 12.0cm	MUAC under 12cm	Total children
children	320	52	28	400
percentage	80%	13%	7%	

Percentage is calculated as follows:

$$\% = \frac{\text{Number of children in that category}}{\text{total number of children}} \times 100$$

Additional information should be given where appropriate, for example:

a) if most of the severely malnourished children are marasmic or have kwashiorkor, or
b) if the majority of the children are only just below 80%, or just above.

4.8. Using the results

The results have three main uses:

i.   to determine the severity of the nutrition problem
ii. to help to identify, among different relief centres in the same area, where the main problems lie and where to direct limited resources
iii. to decide which interventions (if any) should be appropriate and which should have priority

The following Table may be helpful in planning an appropriate response.

Table 6

Survey results	Other factors	Action
Over 20% malnourished	1. Poor general ration 2. None	Improve logistics of general food supplies. Supplementary Feeding for all children and vulnerable groups may be considered if resources permit
10-20% malnourished	1. General ration less than 1,750 Kcals/day 2. Severe Public Health hazards 3. Significant diseases (esp. measles) prevalent 4. None	Selective Feeding Programmes for the malnourished and the 'vulnerable' groups should be implemented
Less than 10% malnourished (less than 2% seriously malnourished)		Supplementary Feeding Programmes may be started but they should not take priority. This may be reviewed if other problems prevail

SURVEILLANCE OF NUTRITION STATUS

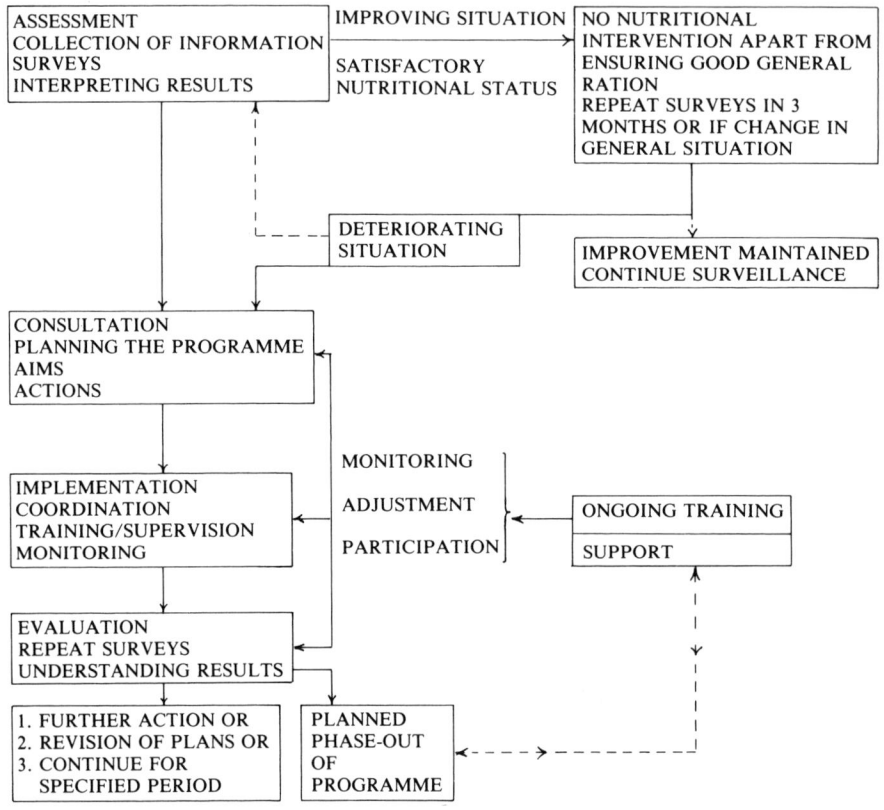

4.9. Repeat surveys

It is useful to repeat surveys periodically, to assess progress and assist with planning.

When the survey is repeated the same houses can be revisited, but it is probably better to select anew as otherwise new arrivals would automatically be excluded from the survey.

PART TWO: SELECTIVE FEEDING PROGRAMMES

CHAPTER 5.

FEEDING PROGRAMMES

There are three types of Programmes to consider:
5.1. General Ration Distribution
5.2. Supplementary Feeding Programme (SFP)
5.3. Therapeutic Feeding Programme (TFP)

5.1. General Ration Distribution

In any emergency, the first priority should be to ensure that enough food is available, i.e. that there is an adequate general ration.

The 'well-nourished' in the community or relief centre will qualify only for a General Feeding Programme; if this basic ration is adequate, it should prevent any deterioration in nutrition status. A general basic ration should aim at providing 1,750 Kilocalories per person per day. (See basic requirements and food tables in Appendix 4.)

Note: If the current emergency has been preceded by a long period of displacement or drought, then 1,750 Kcals/person/day may not be sufficient to promote an early return to good nutritional status. In these situations, it may be advisable to consider issuing a more generous basic ration - 2,000-2,500 Kcals/person/day - if the logistics are manageable.

Usually the general ration distribution is coordinated by the Government administration and international agencies such as World Food Programme (WFP), UNICEF and UNHCR. Non-Governmental Organisations (NGOs) are less likely to be involved, since this tends to be a large operation, often beyond their capacity.

The main problems encountered in General Feeding are logistical ones of transport, storage, stock control and corruption. Inadequate supplies or underestimation of the situation may have serious repercussions.

Table 7: A typical individual daily ration

Commodity	Quantity	Kilocalories
1. A staple food providing the main energy and protein requirement, e.g. cereal	350-400gm	1225-1400
2. A high calorie food, e.g. oil	20-40gm	180-360
3. A protein source, e.g. beans, pulses	50gm	350 (approx.)

5.2. Supplementary Feeding Programmes (SFP)

In a refugee or emergency situation where there is an adequate general ration, Supplementary Feeding should only be necessary to restore good nutritional status in those individuals who are malnourished, and such an SFP should not continue as a long-term programme unless there is a clearly indicated nutritional need. An SFP can also be applied as a preventive measure which aims to maintain or improve the nutritional status of vulnerable groups; but again, this should not be a long-term intervention. The priority should always be establishing a good general ration.

5.2.1. Vulnerable groups

This term refers to those who, because of their age or physical condition, are particularly at risk of becoming malnourished. In addition to a good general ration, they may also benefit from a regular high energy supplement which contains adequate quantities of protein. These groups include:

i. The malnourished

Those whose weight/height (or length) is below 80%, and some borderline cases with additional health problems, e.g. anaemia.

ii. Children under 5 years old

In areas where there are many risk factors (inadequate general ration, poor sanitation and water supplies, measles epidemic, etc.) it may be necessary to consider SFP for *all* children under 5 years old. However, considerable resources and logistic support are necessary for implementation, and this is often not practicable.

As many mothers do not know the exact ages of their children, the simplest method is to identify this group by selecting all those children less than 115cm tall (since the normal average height of a 5 year old is 109cm, this allows a safety margin). A measuring stick or a simple height arch can be used. (See Appendix 6.) Screening equipment is available in the Oxfam Feeding Kits (Appendix 3).

iii. Pregnant women

A pregnant woman needs extra food in order to maintain her own good health and that of her developing baby. This group should be identified and registered - as early as possible in pregnancy - for Supplementary Feeding. Often traditional birth attendants are able to provide invaluable assistance in locating these women since, in practice, many women fraudulently claim to be pregnant in order to qualify for extra rations.

iv. Lactating women

Mothers should be encouraged to breast-feed for as long as possible. Any woman breast-feeding should be eligible to receive supplementary food.

In addition, breast-fed infants who are malnourished (under 80% weight/length) but over 4 months old may be given a small amount of supplementary food.

v. Those discharged from a Therapeutic Feeding Centre (TFC)

Any child discharged from a TFC (or Intensive Feeding Programme) is at particular risk of another episode of malnutrition; these children would have received a high energy diet for several weeks, and a sudden drop in intake is to be avoided. All such children should automatically be referred and registered for the SFP. These children should wear both SFP and TFC identity bracelets as any deterioration in their condition is particularly significant. (See 6.4.4.)

vi. Selected medical cases

Medical cases may be referred from the health centre/post for SFP; most likely to be referred are those individuals suffering from anaemia, tuberculosis, or indeed any wasting which is secondary to other serious illnesses.

vii. Old people

The elderly do not always receive supplementary food, especially if supplies are limited. However, those who are very frail, sick or unable to cope with the general ration - because of lack of teeth or digestive upsets - should be registered for SFP, if resources permit.

Particularly at risk, too, are those separated from their relatives or who live alone.

viii. Social groups

Orphans, unaccompanied minors and those with particular social problems, e.g. the disabled, people living alone, may also be admitted to SFPs.

5.3. Therapeutic Feeding Programmes

Therapeutic (Intensive) Feeding is intended to rehabilitate the most seriously malnourished, e.g. those below 70% weight for height, plus those individuals suffering from oedema. It therefore aims to provide a daily diet which is high in energy, contains adequate amounts of protein, is low in bulk, and is palatable.

The majority of those needing Therapeutic Feeding are also suffering from other illnesses, making medical supervision essential. (See Chapter 7.)

CHAPTER 6.

THE SUPPLEMENTARY FEEDING PROGRAMME (SFP)

6.1. 'Wet' and 'Dry' Supplementary Feeding Programmes

Once the decision has been taken to start a Supplementary Feeding Programme, two main methods of distribution should be considered:

i. on-the-spot or 'wet' ration distribution system which involves distribution of cooked food at Feeding Centres;

ii. take-home or 'dry' ration distribution, which involves the distribution of a ration to be prepared at home by the mother.

Table 9 shows the relative advantages and disadvantages of both methods. However, perhaps the most important factor in deciding which system to adopt is the need to ensure that the supplement does reach those most at risk. *On-the-spot feeding may be more suitable for children.* The dry or take-home ration system may be appropriate for pregnant and lactating women, taking cultural factors into account.

If method (i) is adopted, the necessary cooking equipment may not be available locally. In this situation, the Oxfam Feeding Kits may be appropriate.(See Appendix 3.)

Method (ii) may require the development of a simple ration card - see example in Table 8. These cards can be modified according to specific needs, e.g. to cope with daily, weekly or monthly distribution days. *However, identity bracelets and a register are probably more satisfactory and less likely to be lost. (See 6.4.4.)*

Table 8: Sample Supplementary Ration Card

REGISTRATION NUMBER:	AREA OF RELIEF CENTRE OR SECTION NUMBER			LOCAL LEADER'S NAME				This information should also be recorded in a register to enable follow-up
NAME:								It may also be useful to record name of mother or father
HOME TOWN/VILLAGE:								
AGE:				SEX:				
REGISTRATION DATE	WT	HT	%	COMMENTS				Comments could include: Anaemia, Oedema, Vitamin A — date given etc.

DATE OF RATION DIST.	WT	HT	%	DATE OF RATION DIST.	WT	HT	%	The date ration is distributed can be recorded and the *next* distribution date pencilled in.

This can be modified for pregnant and lactating women, the elderly, etc.

Ration cards often become stained, damaged, torn, etc. If possible they should be protected by a plastic envelope.

Table 9:

Advantages and disadvantages of distribution methods for supplementary foods

FACTORS	TAKE-HOME SYSTEM (DRY RATION)	ON-THE-SPOT SYSTEM (WET OR COOKED RATION)
CONSUMPTION OF FOOD BY RECIPIENT	No guarantee that the intended child/adult receives the food supplement: it may be shared by the whole family, or unfamiliar food might not be eaten. Good monitoring is essential.	The ration is consumed under supervision. Assistance can be given to those too ill or unable to eat.
DEGREE OF INTERVENTION	Lower, because fewer distribution days require fewer resources. Less supervision necessary. Home-based records or ration cards needed.	Higher degree of assistance needed, higher costs, more facilities and equipment. More staff needed and may strain resources in terms of water, firewood etc.
TEACHING	Less opportunity generally but need to demonstrate recipes for unfamiliar relief foods. May be possible to promote use of enriched local produce. Opportunities *do* exist for home follow-up and teaching at home with mother taking full responsibility for her own child.	Mothers can assist in food preparation. Children eat under supervision. Both individual and community problems may become apparent earlier and thus can be dealt with sooner.
LOGISTICS	Greater flexibility as the ration can be distributed weekly, fortnightly or monthly.	Less flexibility — feeding may take place twice daily. Some mothers may find it difficult to attend.
DISTANCE	Distance of recipients from Centres is less critical.	Important: Centres must be localised and easily accessible.
CULTURAL	Usually traditional to prepare food in family groups.	Usually contrary to many cultures and beliefs, e.g. in some countries women must not be seen eating in public.
TRAINING	Less training needed for field workers, but strong emphasis needed on supervision.	Need to train refugee and relief workers in management, food preparation and follow-up.
OTHER OPPORTUNITIES	May be restricted but this method tends to be less disruptive to family life.	Feeding Centres may act as focal points for other activities. e.g. community meetings, immunisations etc.; also as a focus for improved monitoring.

A phased closure of a Supplementary Feeding Centre (SFC) may involve a change from wet ration or on-the-spot feeding to a take-home system.

6.2. Daily supplementary requirements

The size of the daily supplement will depend on the general situation.

Table 10

	SITUATION	KCALS/DAY
(a)	Supplement for moderately malnourished, assuming that there is an adequate general ration.	300-500 Kcals/child/day
(b)	Supplement when general ration provides less than 1500 Kcals/person/day	500-1000 Kcals/day

Suitable local foods should be used, if available. (See Appendix 5 for recipes.)

6.3. Selection

Criteria for selection varies in different situations, therefore the guidelines given below are adaptable. It is important that the same criteria for selection are used in all sections of any one camp. Ideally this should be standardised for all camps, and at national and/or international level.

It is not always the most needy people who ask for food: *often it is those who are strong enough to get to the Centre for the selection procedures while the weakest remain hidden in their shelters. It is important for health workers to look around each house, tent, or shelter at frequent intervals.* It is often during these hunts that one finds the most seriously malnourished lying in the darkest corners, under bundles of rags; these are usually the ones that have been given up by their families, and they should be brought for assessment with their siblings.

6.3.1. Rapid screening method

All children in the camp should be weighed and measured, although this may not be possible if the camp is large. The camp leader may be asked to bring all the thin children to a central area for weighing and measuring; or house-to-house searches by health workers can be organised and all children under 5 years old with a MUAC of less than 14cm can then be accompanied to the central area for weighing and measuring. Any older individuals who are obviously malnourished can also be referred.

6.3.2. Selection by weight for height

Any child of less than 80% of standard weight for height is malnourished and in need of Supplementary Feeding. Any child of less than 70% of standard weight/height should be considered for Therapeutic Feeding wherever possible. Any child of less than 60% of standard weight/height is in a very serious condition and unlikely to survive without very special care.

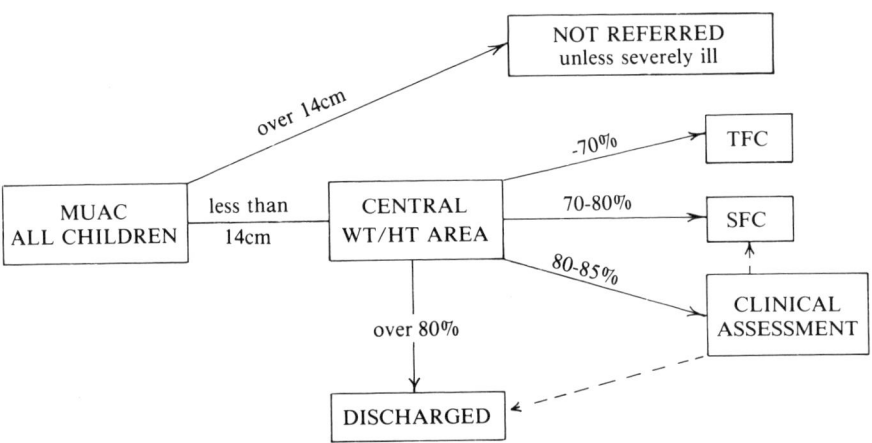

MUAC is suitable for initial screening but admission should be based on weight/height.

6.3.3. General points - coverage

Whichever screening method is used, it is important that all the relief centres are covered and that newcomers are seen on arrival. The nutritional status of children not admitted to the SFP should also be checked periodically by repeated nutritional surveys and home visiting.

Virtually all this screening can be carried out by members of the community, each of whom takes responsibility for a given number of dwellings or families (say 100). Usually the community is divided administratively into sections or groups and it is essential to work through these structures, and to cooperate with those already involved in community work such as traditional healers and birth attendants, teachers, community health workers, traditional leaders, etc.

6.4. Organisation of the Programme (on-the-spot feeding)

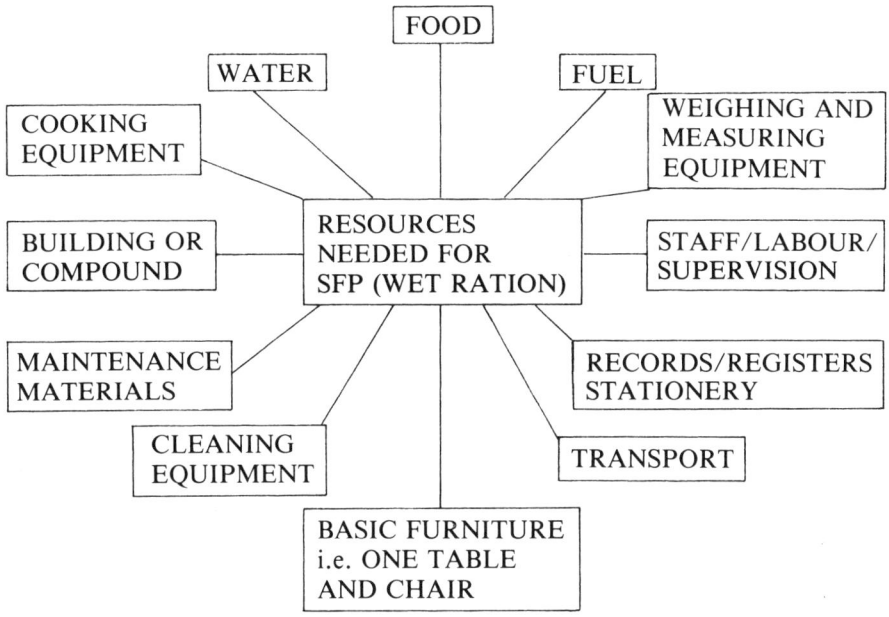

Supplementary Feeding Centres can and should be managed by members of the community. Refugee committees could take responsibility for selecting Centre staff and it may be advisable for all staff handling food to undergo a basic health check.

Agencies must not undertake compensation of Feeding Programme workers, without consultation and coordination with the Government or lead agency. In order to establish a common policy on this difficult issue, inter-agency cooperation is essential.

Good supervision is vital for the Programme to be effective, and it is therefore advisable to keep the Centres to a manageable size: the maximum number of children in each Centre should not exceed 500, but 250 is a much easier number to manage. Rather than establishing one large Centre, it is better to have several smaller Centres servicing a particular area of a camp, and a greater degree of community participation is then also possible.

The minimum facilities needed would be a cleared compound with some shade, e.g. a large tree or thatch roof. The kitchen area should be protected by a low fence in order to prevent accidents occurring, such as burns or scalds. Alternatively, a large empty building can be used.

When discussing possible locations with community leaders, it is useful to bear in mind the following:

i. fuel source
ii. water source
iii. storage space
iv. record-keeping and personnel
v. proximity to the people

6.4.1. Fuel

Usually the local form of fuel (e.g. wood or charcoal) is adequate initially, and it is normal for parents to contribute this; but the sudden increase in the population in the area may put a strain on the normal sources of supply, so that it becomes necessary to travel further and further afield to gather enough stocks. Whatever type of fuel is being used, the workers should be aware of the need for economy in order to conserve supplies. Alternatively, locally constructed mud-brick stoves or other appropriate technologies may help to conserve valuable fuel.

6.4.2. Water

Similar problems may arise over water supplies. Often there is no clean, piped water supply at the Feeding Centres and it will be necessary to arrange collection, storage and treatment of adequate quantities each day. This often comes straight from a river or well and can be stored in clean oil-drums or similar containers. (Advice on the storage and treatment of water is available in the Oxfam Field Directors' Handbook and Ross Bulletins Nos. 8 and 10.) Water needs to be available for cooking and washing-up. If at all possible, the children should wash their hands, and a bucket, cup and soap should be provided for the purpose.

Where water problems are severe, the Oxfam Water Kit (extraction, storage and treatment of water) may be appropriate.

6.4.3. Storage

Suitable, secure storage must be arranged for food supplies and cooking utensils. A watchman (or two!) may need to be employed night and day.

6.4.4. Registration and record-keeping

All those people selected for Supplementary Feeding should be registered. It is useful to weigh all the malnourished, the sick and those children discharged from Intensive Feeding. These people can then be re-weighed regularly (e.g. every two weeks) to assess their progress.

When filling in the register it is useful to record basic information, e.g. registration number, name, age, sex, arm circumference, weight, height, percentage weight for height and other general comments like oedema, anaemia etc. Where possible the child's home, or at least the area of the camp, should be listed in order to assist in tracing defaulters from the Feeding Programme.

In order to re-identify these groups for follow-up weighing, it is necessary to issue them with individual identity bracelets or cards. Bracelets can be attached to the ankles of small babies or to the wrists of older children and adults. These should be marked with the Feeding Centre and the registration number of the individual.

The advantage of these bracelets is that they are not easily removed or lost and therefore make follow-up weighing more rapid and reliable. They also help to ensure that the right people receive the ration. However, bracelets do get lost and exchanged!

6.5. Procedures for Supplementary Feeding

6.5.1. Food supplies should be collected from the store before each meal. The food should be prepared by cooks under the supervision of a responsible member of the community.

6.5.2. Some loud, recognisable sound (e.g. a bell, gong etc.) should be made ten minutes before each meal to summon the children to the compound.

6.5.3. As people arrive they should wash their hands in water provided outside the compound. However, where there is an acute water shortage it is not always possible to provide this facility.

6.5.4. Before entering the compound all bracelets and cards must be checked and the children weighed if necessary. Attendance should be recorded on the register, although if large numbers are involved, this may not be practicable. A head-count may be the only feasible option.

Any new admissions to the Programme should be weighed, measured, registered and given a bracelet.

6.5.5. It may be feasible to provide some seating arrangements e.g. benches or mats.

6.5.6. Food should be served punctually at the appointed time. Any latecomers should be hurried into the compound and the gate closed.

6.5.7. The food should be served by kitchen workers, using a suitable measure; it should be put into clean utensils either belonging to the people themselves or provided specifically for this purpose.

6.5.8. The supervisor and assistants should pass among the people checking that each one has received food and encouraging children to eat the full ration. They should give assistance to mothers and attendants as necessary.

6.5.9. After eating their food the people should leave by a different gate from the one through which they entered, placing - in a receptacle provided for that purpose - any plates, cups or spoons belonging to the Programme. There must be an attendant at this gate to ensure that no food is taken out of the compound.

6.5.10. In some cases there may be a reason why a person in need of extra food cannot attend Supplementary Feeding. Each of these cases should be investigated individually and a note or special card issued to allow a relative to collect the ration.

6.5.11. At the end of each meal and before being stored, all utensils, cups, plates and buckets should be washed and counted by the supervisor. It is advisable to boil the water for the next meal at this stage or earlier, so that it can cool.

6.5.12. The Feeding Programme should be coordinated with other health measures such as immunisation, education, screening for Vitamin A deficiency and anaemia, and simple curative treatments. In areas where Vitamin A deficiency is common, all children should be given an oral supplement (see Chapter 8).

6.5.13. In practice this means discussing all feeding policies with Government authorities and camp leaders, and coordinating activities and planning. *As far as possible the aim should be to make the organisation and running of Supplementary (and to a lesser extent Therapeutic) Feeding the responsibility of camp committees.*

6.6. Follow-up weighing

Poor weight gain in individuals should be investigated for signs of underlying illness and the need for Therapeutic Feeding may be considered. The homes of these problem children should be visited, preferably by a responsible member of the refugee community or Feeding Centre attendant.

An overall trend towards poor weight gain among the recipients of the supplementary ration is a more serious problem and should lead to a thorough investigation of the effectiveness of the General Feeding Programme, the efficiency of the distribution system and *the suitability of the diet provided. The food prepared at the SFC should also be checked in these circumstances.*

Children should be re-weighed regularly (e.g. every two weeks) and, at the end of each weighing session, the number of children losing weight, staying the same, or gaining weight should be added up and expressed in percentages.

If the Supplementary Feeding Programme is successful there should be a rapid decline - certainly after 6-8 weeks - in the number of children needing Therapeutic Feeding. Children who drop out, or fail to appear for re-weighing, should be followed up by a home visit.

6.7. Discharge

Children can be discharged from Supplementary Feeding when they are free from obvious disease, active, have a good appetite and more than 85% weight/height on two consecutive weighings.

6.8. Other activities at Supplementary Feeding Centres.

i. Health education.

ii. Referral.

   It is necessary to establish a referral system between TFC, SFC, preventive, curative and follow-up services.

Where the patients and children are gathered at Supplementary Feeding Centres this is a good opportunity for other health inputs. In particular, teaching is possible on some subjects such as preparation of relief foods, immunisation, protection of water supplies, refuse disposal and other environmental measures.

6.9. Problems

The main problems of Supplementary Feeding are:

i. Poor attendance

ii. Failure of children to gain weight; this is usually due to factors such as:
    - inadequacy of the General Feeding Programme
    - miscalculation of formulae or 'diversion' of supplies while making up the formula
    - unequal distribution of food within the family
    - poorly organised and supervised Programme
    - illness or loss of appetite.

   It should be emphasised that supplementary rations are a supplement and NOT a substitute for the normal general ration.

6.10.Criteria for closing Supplementary Feeding

i. Where the number of malnourished is significantly reduced, e.g. less than 10% of children under 5 years old, it may be of more use to manage these individuals from other health or community services facilities, if the following criteria are satisified:

- General Feeding Programme is reliable and adequate
- Public Health and disease control measures are effective
- no seasonal deterioration in health conditions can be anticipated

ii. Take-home rations or day-care facilities or home visiting 'nutrition scouts' may be used to monitor the remaining malnourished or vulnerable individuals during the phasing-out stage.

iii. Follow-up surveys must be planned to ensure that any deterioration does not go unnoticed. This is especially important if the overall situation remains unstable (for example, likely to give rise to a new influx of people or a break-down in supplies).

CHAPTER 7.

THERAPEUTIC FEEDING PROGRAMMES

7.1. Introduction

The purpose of Therapeutic Feeding is to attempt to rehabilitate those children who are so malnourished that they are unlikely to survive unless treated intensively with special foods.

As children admitted to the TFC are likely to be suffering from a concurrent illness, good medical care is also necessary.

Because of these factors, Therapeutic Feeding can become dependent on considerable expatriate involvement. However, it *is* possible to organise adequate Therapeutic Feeding with less expatriate input than has been usual.

Table 12(1) shows some of the possible alternatives which may be considered.

Table 12(1)

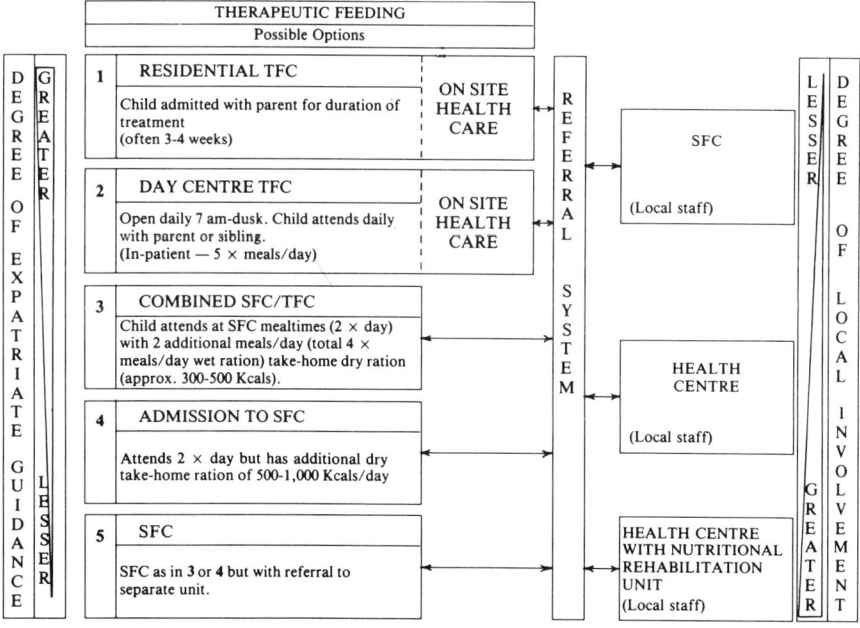

In recent disasters Options 1 or 2 have been chosen, which place considerable emphasis on professional resources. Options 3 and 4 have been successfully used in other situations where resources are limited; but good monitoring is essential. Option 5 is possible if numbers are small and located near an existing Government Nutritional Rehabilitation Unit; it has been successfully used recently but will only be fully effective if patients are followed up after discharge.

Table 12(2): Therapeutic Feeding

OPTIONS	ADVANTAGES	DISADVANTAGES
1.	Encourages attendance and regular supervision of feeds. Earlier detection of potential problems. Easier monitoring of progress. Concurrent Health and Nutritional Care. This offers the best chance of recovery. Mortality rates can usually be kept to less than 10% of children under treatment.	Disrupts family life in that the mother and child are separated from the rest of the family often for up to 30 days or more. Needs fairly intensive medical supervision by experienced Nurse or Doctor.
2.	Allows more flexibility than Option 1.	Lack of night feeds may slow down rate or reduce chances of recovery. Child may not attend regularly and some disruption to family life is inevitable.
3. 4.	Mother is free to spend more time with rest of the family. May cause less disruption to family life. Less expatriate involvement needed.	No guarantee that the supplement will reach the intended beneficiary. Good monitoring is essential. Lack of supervision significantly reduces the likelihood of recovery.
5.	May have access to diagnostic facilities e.g. laboratory.	May overwhelm existing health facilities or take child and relative away from relief centre (in some cases, this could be an advantage).

7.2. Daily Therapeutic requirements

Therapeutic Feeding should provide the *total* amount of calories needed by the patient. To do this it is necessary to make a *high energy, low bulk, palatable food* with an adequate protein, vitamin and mineral content, which can be taken in the necessary volumes by children of all ages. The most readily available bases for energy foods are milk, sugar and oil. There are many products available for this purpose but it is often necessary to make a simple High Energy Milk formula (HEM) from the basic ingredients (a recipe for a HEM can be found in Appendix 5).

Therapeutic Feeding must provide AT LEAST FOUR FEEDS, and ideally six or seven feeds daily of a formulated high energy mixture.

A strong emphasis must be placed on the importance of breast-feeding and, where this has failed, on the re-establishment of lactation.

7.2.1. Nutritional aims of a Therapeutic Feeding Programme

The aim is to give each severely malnourished child at least 150 Kilocalories (Kcals) plus 3-4gm protein/Kilogram body weight/day. The ideal HEM must have at least 1Kcal in every millilitre (ml), thus 100ml of HEM contains 100Kcals.

Using this formula it is easy to work out the requirements of HEM for children of different weights. The volume of HEM given at each feed will depend on the frequency of the feeding, as defined in Table 13.

Table 13

Weight of child	Vol. and energy requirement.	Vol. required for each feed @ 4 feeds/day	Vol. required for each feed @ 5 feeds/day	Vol. required for each feed @ 6 feeds/day
less than 5Kg	750ml = 750Kcals	200ml	150ml	150ml
5.0-7.5Kg	1125ml = 1125Kcals	300ml	250ml	200ml
7.5-10.0Kg	1500ml = 1500Kcals	400ml	300ml	250ml
10.0-12.5Kg	1875ml = 1875Kcals	500ml	400ml	300ml
For children over 12.5Kg give at least 500ml at each feed.				

These figures are approximate but give some guide to a child's individual needs.

Malnourished children (particularly those with kwashiorkor) are likely to run a risk of potassium depletion, especially if they have diarrhoea, which can be common during the first few days of re-establishing feeding. If available, potassium chloride can be given: a bulk solution can be prepared using 7.5gm in 100ml water, and the child can be given 5ml/Kg of body weight daily in divided doses, added to the feeds.

A simpler alternative is to use the prepackaged ORS (oral rehydration salts) in the recommended solution, to provide additional drinks.

WARNING DO NOT make the milk solution *too* concentrated as the resulting high levels of salt (NaCl) may prove lethal. The recipes shown in Appendix 5 produce safe levels.

7.2.2. Feeding schedule

A regular schedule for Therapeutic Feeding is essential. To obtain good results all feeds must be served punctually and at reasonable intervals.

Local foods should be introduced into the Programme as soon as possible according to the progress of each individual. Small children will find that about six milk feeds per day are all that they can cope with. However, larger children will require additional foods to satisfy their appetites. These should be introduced soon after their arrival at a TFC.

7.2.3. Suggested High Energy feeding schedule for in-patients

6 a.m.   9 a.m.   12 noon   3 p.m.   6 p.m.   9 p.m.   12 midnight.

Where adequate staff and facilities are available a late-night feed should be given at about 12 midnight. This is particularly important for the most severe cases of PEM (see Hypoglycaemia/Hypothermia).

7.2.4. Suggested High Energy feeding schedules for out-patients

7-8 a.m.   11-12 noon   2-3 p.m.   6-7 p.m.

It is useful to introduce alternative foods into the out-patients' schedule. For example, Instant Corn Soya Milk (ICSM) (see recipes in Appendix 5) can be given to add some variety to the child's diet. This can be prepared with oil to give a higher energy content. The porridge may be given twice a day with the first and last feeds.

7.2.5. Re-establishment of lactation

Breast-feeding should be encouraged for as long as possible, but it is essential during the first six months and ideally should continue for at least twelve months.

When lactation has failed, it is important to try to re-establish breast-feeding in the mother or female relative caring for the child:

a) put the infant to the breast for about five minutes at least every two or three hours;
b) give aditional feeds (to mother and child) until the milk supply is established;
c) if necessary, give the mother chlorpromazine 25mg three times daily for ten days. This will encourage the 'let down' reflex.

7.3. Admission procedure for a Therapeutic Feeding Centre

(Procedures for admission to the TFC and the organisation of the food distribution will be described as for in-patient programmes but all procedures will need to be adapted to different situations.)

i. Any child under 70% of standard weight for height should be admitted to the Centre, but where facilities are very limited this may not be possible and clinical judgement must be used to select those most in need.
Usually any child with kwashiorkor or oedema is admitted regardless of its weight for height. Any child in need that cannot be registered for Therapeutic Feeding, should be admitted to the Supplementary Feeding Centre. Later admissions to the TFC may include those referred from SFC because of persistent failure to gain weight, when obvious causes have been ruled out.

ii. An attendant (e.g. parent, brother or sister) must accompany any very young or very sick child, and consent must always be obtained.

iii. A space with a mat should be found in the Centre. Alternatively, the family may prefer to supply their own resting mat.

iv. All admissions should be recorded in the TFC register with the registration number, name, age and sex of the child; the child should be given an identity bracelet with the corresponding number.

v. The register should also record the child's weight, height, arm circumference and approximate age.

vi. The child should be given a milk card with his name and number marked and the volume of milk he is to receive at each feed. It is often easiest to make this in the form of a picture and hang it over the child's sleeping area. (These cards are available in Oxfam Feeding Kit No. 3.) The volume should be increased as the child gains weight (see Table 13). Therefore after re-weighing, all feeding cards should be altered to indicate the new volumes as required.

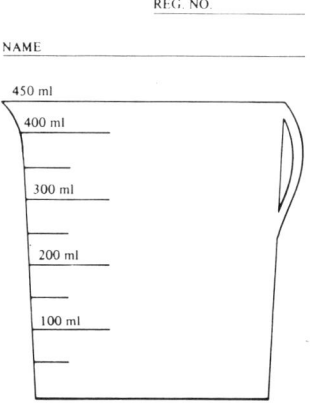

vii. The feeding procedure must be carefully explained to the mother/attendant, stressing the fact that food is the treatment.

Isolation: Since infectious diseases (especially gastro-enteritis, measles, meningitis and pertussis) so often prove fatal to the undernourished child, it is useful if all admissions to the TFC can be *isolated* for the first few days of their treatment. This is also useful where there are screening facilities for TB. In the overcrowded conditions usually prevailing in a disaster situation there is a very real danger of widespread epidemics. Measles immunisation is a priority and ideally should be given within two days of admission to a TFC (if not effected during mass 'camp' immunisation).

7.4. Organisation of the Programme

The procedures described below cover in-patient treatment under basic conditions. Where other facilities - such as access to a laboratory - are available these will be of great help to the TFC.

7.4.1. Location and numbers

An empty building with a compound is ideal, although a simple, weatherproof shelter can be constructed fairly easily. The ideal number of children in a Centre would be 50-60. The absolute maximum should be 100, as adequate supervision then becomes very difficult and there is a real danger of the spread of communicable diseases.

7.4.2. Training

Some training is required for local staff working in a TFC, and they must be supervised by trained health personnel.

7.4.3. Important considerations

i. the cooperation of mothers and workers in the management of the Programme

ii. good supervision of meals

iii. a regular feeding schedule

iv. mats for child and attendant

v. an adequate water supply and/or water storage system

vi. sanitation facilities; if these are not already available, a simple latrine(s) can be constructed. (Advice on sanitation, latrine digging, etc. can be found in the Oxfam Field Directors' Handbook, Ross Institute Bulletin.)

7.5. The feeding procedures in a TFC

7.5.1. The cooks should start preparing the food half-an-hour before it is to be served. They should be supervised by a responsible person.

7.5.2. The hot milk should then be poured into buckets and taken into the eating area.

7.5.3. A responsible person should serve the milk from a clean measuring cup into clean feeding cups, checking that each child is receiving the correct amount according to his or her card.

New admissions should be given half-strength milk for the first 24-48 hours, especially if they have diarrhoea. In these cases oral rehydration salts (ORS) should be encouraged and milk feeds gradually introduced as soon as possible.

7.5.4. The parent or a relative should take responsibility for feeding and supervising their children, with support from the staff.

7.5.5. During the meal all assistants must check that the milk is being taken by the correct child (not by the parent or the siblings). They should give assistance to those parents with children who have poor appetites.

7.5.6. Assistants must insist that each child finishes the complete ration and must report any child who is unable to take his entire feed. The person in charge should take note of any children who are difficult to feed and allocate attendants to assist them.

7.5.7. No child must be rushed. Feeding is a slow, laborious task, especially initially with seriously malnourished children. Other activities should be suspended during meal times.

7.5.8. At the end of each feed all cups, plates and other utensils should be collected, then washed, counted and stored in a clean, covered container or on shelves.

NOTE: *INFANT FEEDING BOTTLES MUST NEVER BE USED IN A THERAPEUTIC FEEDING CENTRE.*

7.5.9. Mothers, siblings and attendants at the TFC should receive the normal ration from the General Feeding Programme and may qualify for the Supplementary Feeding Programme. It is important to ensure that ration distribution times are coordinated to minimise disruption to other Programmes.

7.6. Follow-up and records.

7.6.1. Weighing

Children should be weighed at least twice weekly. Where facilities are available to measure serum albumen levels, these will be found to rise steadily as the child's condition improves and are useful to reinforce other clinical findings.

7.6.2. Observing progress

As the child improves he will become less apathetic and irritable and more physically active. After a few days of treatment the skin condition will improve and by the time of discharge should have returned to its normal, healthy, glowing colour. Usually the open skin lesions of kwashiorkor will heal without specific treatment unless they have become infected.

7.6.3. Records

The Therapeutic Feeding Register should be used to record information about the patients, and the follow-up.

i. All the data must be accurate and up-to-date, and all admissions, transfers, discharges and deaths must be recorded in the register.

ii. If families leave the Centre without being discharged they should be considered absent but not discharged - these families often return to the Centre within a few days. These children should be traced and followed up if absence persists. Where possible, tracing should be carried out by members of the community, ideally from the same area of the camp.

7.7. Assessment of individual patients and discharge procedure from a TFC

The progress of the malnourished child will usually be assessed according to the loss of oedema (in kwashiorkor) and a subsequent steady gain in weight. The aim is to make this growth rate as rapid as possible and to be able to discharge the child from the Programme within 30 days of admission.

Children receiving Therapeutic Feeding should be re-weighed at least twice weekly and individual records kept: this record should be summarised to show:

i. the numbers and percentage falling within each weight group
ii. the numbers gaining weight
iii. the numbers losing weight
iv. the numbers dying
v. the numbers admitted (and re-admitted)

vi. the numbers discharged
vii. those taking their own discharge against advice
viii. those lost to follow-up

In kwashiorkor there is normally an initial loss in weight as the oedema decreases, followed by a steady weight increase similar to the marasmic patient. A failure to lose weight in the early stages of treatment should be noticed with particular attention as this may indicate the onset of congestive cardiac failure. Similarly, any signs of drowsiness or loss of consciousness may be suggestive of cerebral oedema.

In summary, before discharge from a Therapeutic Feeding Centre a child should be active, healthy, gaining weight steadily *and at least 80% of standard weight for height.*

A member of the health team should examine each child before discharge. *Each child discharged from the Centre should be referred to his nearest Supplementary Feeding Programme* for continued care. He should continue to wear his TFC bracelet in addition to his SFC bracelet.

All discharges should be recorded in the register.

Where possible children should be followed up in routine home visits for three months; alternatively, they can be followed up through SFC.

7.8. Other activities at Therapeutic Centres.

Opportunities for health education will exist; however, as many children in Therapeutic Feeding Centres also have a concurrent illness, activities must be coordinated with monitoring of individual progress, referral and treatment of medical conditions. (See Chapter 8.) The immunisation of young children against measles is a priority because of the high mortality associated with this disease in a malnourished population.

7.9. Other problems associated with Therapeutic Feeding

These problems fall into two categories:
i. Conflict with traditional practices.
ii. Feeding problems.

7.9.1. Conflict

One of the most common and difficult problems to overcome in a TFC is the suspicion found among relatives of the malnourished children of the techniques used in Therapeutic Feeding.

Often food is given at a time when a relative would withhold food, e.g. if the child is unwell. Often, too, an unwilling child needs to be coaxed to take his food where a relative might traditionally feel that this was not important. Endless patience and explanations are necessary to overcome this conflict and to avoid misunderstandings.

Parents and relatives usually prefer medicine and injections, and are doubtful of the therapeutic value of food. However, once the children start improving this problem largely solves itself, since the relatives of recovering children quickly lend support to the argument that food is the best medicine. Ideally such successful relatives should be incorporated as workers in the Programme.

It is more difficult to overcome the distrust aroused by intravenous infusions, naso-gastric tube-feeding and other more frightening procedures, and it is only with firm but sympathetic cooperation with relative and child that these procedures can be carried out.

Inevitably, there will be a number of deaths at the TFC, but it is important that it does not get the reputation of a 'death centre' as this will act as a deterrent and parents will stop bringing their children.

7.9.2. Feeding problems

The problem of anorexia among children admitted to a TFC is a serious one. Mothers have to be told that, however reluctant a child is to eat, she/he must be forced to do so or death will almost certainly occur. Once a child has taken a few feeds she/he will quickly regain an appetite and feeding will become a simple task.

Where encouragement and coaxing have failed, more determined persuasion may have to be used to feed a difficult child. This takes time and patience as, drop by drop, a whole feed is spooned into the unwilling child.

Where a child is very sick or weak, or totally refusing to take his feeds, a naso-gastric tube can be used. In most cases tube feeding is not necessary for more than 24-48 hours. The tube may be left in situ or removed and replaced at each feed. This is also useful when persistent vomiting is the main problem. Small, frequent (hourly) feeds can be introduced.

7.10. Closure of a TFC

If the general ration distribution and Supplementary Programmes are working well, and public health hazards are under control, it should be possible to close the Therapeutic Centre. Where populations are static, this could be within three months.

If numbers attending and new admissions are in decline, it is probably not justified to continue such a Centre for, say, only twenty to thirty children who have not gained weight; such children would probably be better served through existing health structures with good supervision and follow-up at home, as they will have an underlying problem requiring more than Therapeutic Feeding.

The closure of the Therapeutic Centre, if not achieved earlier, should be part of the phased withdrawal from the camp.

CHAPTER 8.

HEALTH CARE FOR PATIENTS ON THERAPEUTIC FEEDING

8.1. General

Medical care is of great importance for children in a TFC since almost all those admitted to such a Centre have some underlying disease. Wherever possible a doctor or nurse should visit each TFC daily and should examine all new admissions to advise on treatment. Any child who is not responding to treatment, or whose condition is deteriorating, should be examined at this time. Any treatment ordered should be clearly marked on a Medical Record card.

It is obviously very helpful for the medical team to be able to make use of laboratory facilities when they are at hand, but a team is rarely so fortunate and usually a clinical diagnosis has to be relied on. It may be feasible to refer children, but care must be taken not to overwhelm existing health structures.

8.1.1. Local health problems

It is essential to assess local health problems, especially the prevalence of communicable diseases and tropical fevers, as these are likely to increase in crowded situations where hygiene is poor. Tuberculosis in particular is a common cause of failure to thrive.

Those running the Programme should be well briefed and have the necessary books and information at their disposal, and should refer to local consultants, if possible.

Simple, safe medicines may be left with trained non-professionals at the Centre with clear, standardised instructions as to their use. A supply of dressings is also useful. (See 'Oxfam's Practical Guide to Refugee Health Care'.)

8.1.2. Use of antibiotics and vaccines

There is a difference of opinion concerning the use of prophylactic antibiotics for all children admitted to a TFC, although some trials show that this may be worth while; any decision must be taken locally.

Where measles vaccine is available all children should be immunised *before* admission (unless they have just had the disease), or within two days of admission.

If in doubt, immunise against measles

8.2. Specific health problems

8.2.1. Fevers

Wherever a diagnosis is made, specific treatment should of course be given. Often, however, this is impossible as the clinical picture may be typical of several diseases - e.g. malaria, typhoid, typhus, flu - and no sophisticated diagnosis aids are available. It is often necessary to give a very broad treatment for an undiagnosed fever, for example:

i. a broadspectrum antibiotic

ii. an anti-malarial

iii. an antipyretic

The incidence of *septicaemia* is high among severe cases of PEM.

8.2.2. Diarrhoea, vomiting (and dehydration)

Children taking a High Energy Milk diet often suffer from diarrhoea, especially during the early stages of treatment. Mothers should be told that this is a normal occurrence and will resolve within a few days *but that feeding should continue as usual*. Additional drinks of ORS can be given.

Lactose Intolerance is an occasional problem in areas where milk is not a normal part of the diet, and should always be considered in cases of persistent diarrhoea. The appearance of the typical stool with a PH of less than 6 (using Litmus paper) indicates the necessity for a change of diet. Often it is only necessary to reduce the milk intake for a few days and then increase it slowly for it to be well tolerated. In cases where intolerance continues, a milk-free diet can be made, usually based on a cereal/oil/sugar mixture, with fish, eggs or meat added if and when possible.

Where vomiting occurs with the diarrhoea it is useful to dilute the HEM by 50% for 24 hours, and give additional drinks of ORS. A careful watch must be kept on the child for signs of dehydration.

When diarrhoea or vomiting persists to the extent that the child is losing weight, other possible causes should be considered. All cases of dysentery (i.e. diarrhoea with blood and mucus) should be treated with an antibiotic if thought to be bacterial, or with amoebicides and antihelminthics (anti-worm) if thought to be parasitic. (See 'Oxfam's Practical Guide to Refugee Health Care'.)

Dehydration: it must be recognised by anyone working in a TFC that dehydration is one of the most common causes of death in malnourished children; it is simple to cure if recognised early enough. The appearance of a dry, loose skin, sunken eyes and a dry mouth should never be overlooked by the local workers but should be reported to the medical personnel as soon as possible. There may be some difficulty in differentiating this from marasmus; often both occur together. Weight for height may help but, if in doubt, assume the child is both dehydrated and marasmic.

Management of dehydration: most cases of dehydration can be treated rapidly by giving large enough quantities of oral fluids. Where nothing else is available, clean water can be given. This, however, does not replace the salts which are lost in diarrhoea and vomiting. It is possible to make a very useful rehydration mixture by adding salt and sugar in the following proportions:

Water	Sugar	Salt
1 litre (boiled and cooled)	8 level teaspoonfuls	1 level teaspoonful

Local flavouring (e.g. orange juice, cinnamon etc.) can be added for palatability.

This mixture can be given by cup, by spoon, or by naso-gastric tube. If a child is vomiting persistently, all other foods should be stopped and this mixture given in small amounts every quarter-of-an-hour. Where dehydration has resulted from high fever, diarrhoea, or lack of adequate water supplies it is advisable to continue both high energy feeds and the rehydration mixture until improvement is seen.

A severely dehydrated child may require an intravenous, rectal or intraperitoneal infusion. This applies especially if vomiting continues.

To cover all *normal* requirements a child needs 100-150ml/Kg body weight, depending on age, PLUS the replacement for any loss due to diarrhoea, vomiting or excessive perspiration occurring with high fever. *Progress is best measured by weighing the child*, a gain in weight indicating successful treatment.

Those children being rehydrated should be examined hourly to check that their condition has not deteriorated and that the relative is giving the necessary volume of oral rehydration mixture. To facilitate this, the children are best identified by placing a card over their sleeping area with a suitable sign or colour.

Clean drinking water should always be available for general consumption, particularly in hot climates.

Table 14: Fluid requirements for dehydrated children

Dehydration	Indication	Treatment
Mild	Weight loss less than 5%. Skin elasticity slightly less than normal. Eyes, normal or slightly sunken. Restless and thirsty.	Oral rehydration salts 120ml/Kg body weight. Can be given at home over 4-6 hours. Continue until improvement is maintained.
Moderate		Oral rehydration salts, via naso-gastric tube if unable to drink well or tolerate oral fluids. 120ml/Kg body weight at frequent intervals for the first 6 hours, under observation.
Severe	More than 5% weight loss. Limp or unconscious. Too weak to drink well. Cold skin. Skin elasticity very poor. Sunken eyes and fontanelle. Little or no urine.	May need intravenous fluids if other methods failed or child is unconscious. Half strength Darrow's solution with 2.5% glucose. 150ml/Kg body weight given over 6 hours (half to be given in the first hour). If given peritoneally, 70ml/Kg body weight can be given in 10-20 minutes instead of 4-6 hours.

8.2.3. Hypothermia and Hypoglycaemia (low body temperature, low blood sugar)

These conditions are common on cool nights in a TFC where patients have a high energy intake for most of the day but none at night. A sudden illness or the onset of vomiting which makes a child unable to take his normal feeds may precipitate a fatal episode of hypoglycaemia.

Prevention:

i. The children should be kept as warm as possible in order to conserve heat and energy. Small children should be held close by their attendants. Very small children can be wrapped in blankets and metal foil or placed in a paper food sack to keep them well insulated. Hot water bottles can be used (with the usual precautions against burns) for very small children.

ii. It is very important to keep the gap between night and morning feeds as short as possible, thereby reducing the danger period. In certain circumstances the mother can be given a night ration for the child.

Treatment:

i. A collapsed child should be kept warm but not heated up rapidly.

ii. Give a concentrated sugar solution (usually in the form of sterile dextrose 50%) either:

a) by mouth, or

b) by naso-gastric tube, or

c) by intravenous injection

It has been found that any child who suffers from such an episode has a poor prognosis even if they appear initially to recover.

8.2.4. Worms

All patients admitted to a TFC should be treated with a suitable antihelminthic preparation when they are in an adequate physical condition, usually after 5-7 days.

8.2.5. Measles

Measles is a common cause of malnutrition in the tropics and a frequent killer if introduced into a malnourished community. It is a great help if all children under 3 years of age and all children admitted to the TFC can be immunised against measles. Effective immunisation necessitates an adequate cold chain which ensures that the vaccine is kept cold from the time it leaves the factory of manufacture to the time of injection.

8.2.6. Tuberculosis

A child with PEM who fails to gain weight on a Therapeutic diet may well have tuberculosis and, where facilities exist, this can be diagnosed by microscopy of the sputum (often difficult in children). In certain circumstances a 'trial of TB therapy' may be indicated but, if the child responds, treatment must be continued until the course is completed. This decision should not be taken lightly and a doctor should be consulted. (See 'Oxfam's Practical Guide to Refugee Health Care' - Appendix 10.)

8.2.7. Respiratory infections

These are common, especially with overcrowding. Often the cause is viral, but classical lobar pneumonia is also common and should be treated with simple antibiotics.

8.2.8. Other infections

Other infections (e.g. of skin and urinary tract) may be present and should also be treated because, in malnourished individuals, such infections can rapidly become more serious and lead to avoidable deaths.

8.3. Treatment regimes

It is useful to have at hand standardised treatment regimes for use by health workers. See Table 15 for recommendations.

Table 15: A guide to drug dosages

Antibiotics	Route	Times/day		0-1yr	1 yr	7 yr	Adults
Ampicillin	oral	4	per dose	62.5mg	125mg	250mg	500mg
	IM	4					
Chloramphenicol*	oral	4	"	12mg/Kg	125mg	250mg	500mg
	IM	4					
Tetracycline*	oral	4	"	62.5mg	62.5mg	125mg	250mg
Penicillin V	oral	4	"	62.5mg	125mg	250mg	500mg
Penicillin G	IM	4	"	15mg/Kg	150mg	300mg	600mg
Penicillin (Procaine)	IM	1	"	0.05mg/Kg	0.5ml	1ml	2ml
Triplopen	IM	1/3 days	"	¼ vial	¼ vial	½ vial	1 vial
Sulphadimidine* (Sulphamethazine)	oral	4	per day		125mg/Kg/day		
Antimalarials							
Chloroquine- Phosphate	oral		First dose repeated after 6hrs,24hrs,36hrs		5mg/Kg per dose to a total of 25mg/Kg		
Chloroquine- Sulphate	IM	1/5 days	5mg/Kg x 5 days				
	IV		5mg/Kg in 150ml or normal Saline SLOWLY repeat in 12 hours				
Anti-helminthics							
Piperazine		Under 2 years	2gm)				
		2-5 years	3gm) Repeat in 2 days if necessary				
		Over 5 years	4gm)				
Bephenium hydroxynaphthoate (Alcopar)		Under 2 years	2.5gm in a single dose				
		Over 2 years	5gm in a single dose				

* Caution should be exercised in giving chloramphenicol and sulpha drugs to premature and small babies. Tetracycline should not be given to pregnant women or children under eight years of age unless there are special indications.

Antituberculosis - Conventional treatment schedule

Age/weight	Intensive Phase (3 months)			Maintenance Phase (6 - 9 months)	
	Strep	Daily INH	Thia	Daily INH	Thia
5-12 yrs 16-29Kg	0.5g	250mg	75mg	250mg	75mg
2-5 yrs 7-15Kg	0.25g	150mg	—	150mg	—

General Note

If there is doubt about **child dosages**, the following table would provide a rough guide:

    1 year old: 25% of adult dose
    3 year old: 33% of adult dose
    7 year old: 50% of adult dose
    12 year old: 75% of adult dose

8.4. Vitamin and mineral deficiencies

Table 16

DEFICIENCY	EARLY INDICATORS	PREVENTION/ PROPHYLAXIS	TREATMENT adult dosages*
Vitamin A (Xerophthalmia)	1. Grossly deficient diet. 2. Over 2% of children under 5 years with eye changes e.g. conjunctival xerosis including Bitot's spots. 3. More than one child per 1,000 with old eye scars or lesions.	1. Adequate Vitamin A in diet. 2. Assessment of diet in early drought or disaster situations. 3. Prophylactic Vitamin A if indicators present: single dose of 200,000 IUs orally will give protection for up to 6 months. 100,000 IUs for children under 1 year.	100,000 IUs of Vitamin A IM followed 24 hours later by oral Vitamin A plus adequate protein intake in diet.
Vitamin B1 (Beriberi)	1. Deficiency in diet. 2. Use of white polished rice or cassava as staple.	1. Daily intake of 1mg of thiamine in diet. 2. Rice for emergency feeding should not be too polished.	50mg thiamine followed by 10mg daily until recovery.
Vitamin B Complex (Pellagra)	Staple consists of maize or sorghum.	1. Daily dietary intake of 15-20mg of niacin. 2. Use of undermilled cereals and possibly legumes in Feeding Programmes.	300mg of niacin orally daily until recovery (usually only a few days).
Vitamin C (Scurvy)	1. Serious lack of fruits & vegetables in diet. 2. Haemorrhagic symptoms in malnourished children.	10mg daily in diet e.g. small tomato or leafy vegetable.	500mg or more daily until recovery.
Vitamin D (Rickets)	1. Poor exposure to sunlight. 2. Any suspect bone deformity in young children.	1. Exposure of body to sunlight	No more than 100,000 IUs in a single dose or 100,000 IUs daily for 10-30 days plus exposure to sunlight (overdose is dangerous).
Iron (Anaemia)	1. Marked pallor of conjunctiva in 2% of children. 2. Multiple nutritional deficiencies and diseases in child population e.g. kwashiorkor, malaria, hookworm.	1. Adequate dietary intake. 2. Malaria and hookworm control and treatment. 3. Iron preparations may be indicated for pregnant and lactating women, but supervision may be difficult under relief conditions.	100-150mg of iron daily in divided doses with 5mg of folic acid; this will need to be maintained for several weeks.

*See General Note on Page 57.

CHAPTER 9.

TRAINING OF COMMUNITY HEALTH WORKERS

There are three main roles for personnel involved in Feeding Programmes:

i. **Expatriate, local or national doctor/senior nurse/nutritionist**
   a) Mainly in a supervisory and training capacity
   b) Overall monitoring and repeat surveys

ii. **Feeding Centre staff**
   a) Cooks and food supervisors
   b) Watchmen and helpers with water supplies, fuel etc.

iii. **Health workers**
   a) To assist in the Centres
   b) Locating of malnourished children
   c) To assist with referral to the Health Services
   d) Follow-up of defaulters and those recently discharged
   e) Assistance with repeat surveys and monitoring

Some of these workers will be selected by the community themselves, others will have already had some basic health training. The role of the expatriate should be to support and consolidate the training programmes, but it is essential that these programmes are at an appropriate level and geared to meet the particular problems of the community.

Course content will therefore vary according to the situation, but should include some of the following components:

Practical experience

a) Weighing and measuring techniques
b) Random surveys
c) Food preparation, food hygiene
d) Feeding children
e) Public health measures, e.g. refuse control etc.
f) Home visits

More formal instruction

a) Prevention and management of malnutrition and normal nutrition - children, pregnant and lactating women
b) Diarrhoea, dehydration, ORS
c) Promotion of breast-feeding
d) Identification of illnesses needing referral
e) Immunisations
f) How to manage a food store (See UNHCR 'Handbook for Emergencies')
g) Specific problems, e.g. anaemia, Vitamin A deficiency

CHAPTER 10.

REPORTING/MONITORING AND EVALUATION OF THE PROGRAMME

It is very important to keep the Government and other agencies informed about the general situation in the relief area: the baseline data which is collected during the initial assessment period can be of great assistance to all in defining an appropriate response. It is invaluable as the basis for the evaluation and progress of the relief programme. (See Checklist in Appendix 1.)

10.1. Reporting

Any dramatic developments will be reported as they occur, but a general review of the situation with up-dating of the statistics should be carried out monthly or bimonthly.

Tables 17 and 18 show possible ways of presenting feeding statistics.

Table 17: Supplementary Feeding Data

Category	No. enrolled (end last month)	Admissions (this month)	Discharges (this month) (over 85%)	Total (end this month)
0-5 years (up to 115cm height) (71-80% standard weight for height)				
Pregnant women (last trimester)				
Lactating women				
TB patients (as necessary)				
Elderly (as necessary)				
Medical referrals				
Others e.g. children 6-14 years of age				
TOTAL				

Number children 0-5 years attending daily

1	2	3	4	5	6	7	8	9	10	11	12	13	14	15
16	17	18	19	20	21	22	23	24	25	26	27	28	29	30	31

(Place slash / in boxes on days when all Feeding Centres closed)

No. of children 0-5 years, who: (a) Lost weight _____
                                 (b) Failed to gain weight _____

Table 18: Intensive Feeding Data

Category	No. enrolled (end last month)	Admissions (this month)	Discharges (this month)	Total (end this month)
0-5 years (up to 115cm height) (less than 70% standard weight for height)				
Children with oedema (or active disease)				
Medical referrals				
Older children (e.g. 6-14 years)				
TOTAL				

Number children 0-5 years attending daily

1	2	3	4	5	6	7	8	9	10	11	12	13	14	15

16	17	18	19	20	21	22	23	24	25	26	27	28	29	30	31

(Place slash / in boxes on days when all Feeding Centres closed)

No of children who died whilst in Intensive Feeding Programme

Week 1 _____ Week 2 _____ Week 3 _____ Week 4 _____

What is the percentage of children (excluding those with oedema) losing weight?

Week 1 _____ Week 2 _____ Week 3 _____ Week 4 _____

10.2 Monitoring and evaluation

Although monthly data collection will show the effectiveness of the Feeding Programme, it will *not* show effectiveness of coverage within the camp, or the overall trend in nutrition status.

It is therefore essential to reassess the Programme at regular intervals, i.e. every three or six months. The Checklist can be used and random nutrition surveys repeated. Decisions regarding the future of the Programme can be based on these reassessments.

It may be necessary, for example:

i. to increase coverage of the Programmes by house-to-house visits, or possibly by relocating Feeding Centres if it is shown that many new arrivals are not attending the Centres.

ii. if an overall improvement is indicated, with no new arrivals, planning the closure of Centres should be considered. (See Sections 6.10 and 7.10.)

In addition to nutritional assessment, wider surveillance is essential. (See 'Oxfam's Practical Guide to Refugee Health Care'.)

Appendix 1

CHECKLIST FOR REFUGEE SITUATIONS

1. DEMOGRAPHY AND BACKGROUND
2. FOOD
3. WATER
4. SANITATION
5. MEDICAL CARE
6. SHELTER
7. LOGISTICS
8. REHABILITATION

1. **Demography and Background**

   Numbers: numbers coming, numbers leaving - forecast.

   Proportions: of men, women and children (0-4, 5-14 years)
   birthrate
   mortality

   Where people have come from - previous occupation and environment

   What provisions do they still have

   Environment of camp

   Season - rainy or dry - future seasons

   Who administers camp - how - what staff are employed

   How well-planned is camp layout and siting

   What degree of community involvement is there - are there camp committees

   What agencies are working there

   How do they co-operate - tensions

2. **Food**

   What is the general state of nutrition in the camp

   Has a simple nutritional survey been done

   Are newcomers in a better state of nutrition than those who have been in the camps for some time

   Is the situation deteriorating or improving

   Is there any evidence of specific nutritional deficiencies (in Xeropthalmia, Anaemia etc).

What is the camp population attitude towards the food provided and the feeding programme in general

What fuel is used for cooking: if wood, is there an adequate supply close by, will it last

How is the camp feeding organised - i.e. distribution, preparation and cooking

What foods are used - where from - how do they relate to the population's normal diet

How many calories per person

How are total food requirements of camp estimated

Food cooked at community or family level

Availability of local foods

Local price of food-stuffs - cattle and staple (maize, sorghum)

Has this altered recently

How many meals a day

Is additional food given to vulnerable groups (selective or supplementary)

    If so, what, how much and to whom

How are people selected for this extra food

Is this food eaten in individual dwellings or 'on the spot' under supervision at a feeding centre

Who runs it

Is there any facility for therapeutic feeding of the severely malnourished

    If so, what, and who runs it

Is a record kept of those receiving special food

Is the progress of malnourished individuals monitored

Is the general nutritional status of the camps monitored - how and how frequently

What are the priority needs in the area of food and nutrition. How can these be met

3. **Water**

How is water supplied to the population, i.e. standpipe, river, tanker etc.

What is its source, i.e. river, well, rain, cistern

Is the source relatively clean and likely to remain so

Is the source adequate at all seasons

How close is the supply brought to the refugee's dwelling

What (approx.) is the consumption rate per head

Is there evidence of a severe water-related disease problem. If so, what (i.e. skin disease, typhoid, diarrhoea etc.)

Is there any danger of contamination from latrines, livestock or (in the case of rivers) other camps upstream

Is the water tested regularly

Is there any system of treatment

If a pump is used, how is it serviced and what contingency plans are there if it breaks down

Are washing facilities provided - where

Where are animals watered

How is water stored in the shelters or houses - what containers are used

Does the community understand the concept of contamination of water supplies both at source and in the home

Is there a health education programme covering water usage

What is the 'chain' of water supply from source to final utilisation

What are the main problems in the chain

4. Sanitation

Is there a sanitation problem

How are excreta and waste disposed of (i.e. family or communal, via pit latrines, water-borne system, cartage or random)

Does it present a health hazard

How well are existing systems maintained and kept clean

Is there evidence of a high level of disease which might be related to poor sanitation (i.e. diarrhoea, worms etc.)

Is there sufficient space to allow for pit latrines to be dug

How close is the water source to the sewage disposal point

What is the normal practice of defecation of the refugee population

How do they view the existing camp system

Is the water table high or low

What is the soil structure, i.e. rocky, sandy etc.

How will different seasons affect existing systems (i.e. flooding)

5. **Medical Care**

What basic health facilities exist in the camp

What are the main disease problems of the camp population

How are they measured - what records are kept

Is there any system of surveillance

Is there an unusually high incidence of communicable diseases (i.e. measles, scabies, TB, diarrhoea)

What factors may be responsible for the various diseases (i.e. housing, water, crowding etc.)

What simple preventative measures could be undertaken to alleviate these problems

What measures are being undertaken already

What maternal and child health services exist in the camp

Are there effective vaccines against the prevalent disease

> If so, is there an adequate immunisation programme (quality, coverage etc.)

Are vaccines kept well refrigerated both in transit to camp and in the camp itself

Is there a need for refrigerators

Is the curative care simple, cheap and relevant

Is the drug supply adequate

Are the drugs relevant to the main diseases

Is the drug list limited to simple essential drugs - standardisation

Do the health workers know how to use them

Are there facilities for oral rehydration (where diarrhoea is causing dehydration)

Who is in charge of the health of the camp; what agencies are helping

What evidence is there of community participation in health care

Is adequate use made of medically trained or trainable refugees

Are they trained to do the right things

Are they supervised

To what degree is the community involved (health committees etc.)

Is there a reasonable health education programme

What records are kept

Are 'at risk' registers kept (i.e. for TB)

How are severely sick people referred for more intensive care - where are they sent

6. **Shelter**

   What is the normal housing of the refugee population
   How are the refugees housed - individual families or community shelters
   How many people per shelter
   Is the shelter adequate
   How are the shelters spaced
   Is camp layout organised in small units (i.e. village or tribal groups)
   Is the administration block sufficient What cooking facilities are provided
   Are materials for building available locally
       What are they
   Is there a fire hazard

7. **Logistics**

   How secure are the deliveries of food to the camp
   Are the storage facilities in the camp adequate
   How many days' food can be stored
   Are the roads open in all weathers
   Are the stores efficiently run - are they locked
   Is there evidence of rats or other wastage
   Is routine rodent control undertaken
   Is food properly stacked, i.e. away from walls
   Is there a record system with regular stock-taking
   What form of transport is used, army, government, aid agency etc.
   What servicing facilities exist for vehicles
   How do the camp personnel communicate with the capital
   Is there a regular feed-back of information
   Is this information used in planning intervention and supplies
   What skills are available in the refugee population (i.e. medical, engineering etc.)
   Are they being employed
   Are refugees being trained (i.e. for simple health and nutritional duties)
   What are the priority needs in the area of transport, storage, communication and staffing

8. **Rehabilitation**

    What are the prospects of the refugees returning or being settled in the host country

    Does the government have detailed plans

    How long is it envisaged the camp will remain

    What skills could the refugees use in the camps (weaving etc.)

    What tools are needed

    Is there enough land to provide gardens for refugees

    What other inputs would be needed (i.e. tools, seeds, livestock, advice etc.)

    What facilities exist for schooling

    Are there teachers in the camp population

    What other inputs are needed

    Are there any adult training programmes

    Is there a need for them

    What recreational facilities are there

    How can these be improved

    What are the traditional games and entertainments of the refugees

    What other steps can be taken to raise camp morale

9. **Summary**

    How serious is the situation

    What are the main problems - list in order of priority

    What is the best way of solving them (alternatives where possible)

    What inputs are needed (cash, supplies, personnel)

    What should be planned for short, mid and long term

    What should be the objectives

    How will progress be monitored

Appendix 2 — WEIGHT FOR LENGTH (Supine) FOR BOTH BOYS AND GIRLS
(NCHS/CDC/WHO REFERENCES — 1982)

Length	Median	85%	80%	75%	70%	60%	Length	Median	85%	80%	75%	70%	60%
49.0cm	3.2kg	2.7kg	2.6kg	2.4kg	2.3kg	1.92kg	67.0cm	7.6kg	6.5kg	6.1kg	5.7kg	5.3kg	4.56kg
49.5	3.3	2.8	2.6	2.5	2.3	1.98	67.5	7.8	6.6	6.2	5.8	5.4	4.74
50.0	3.4	2.9	2.7	2.5	2.4	2.04	68.0	7.9	6.7	6.3	5.9	5.5	4.74
50.5	3.4	2.9	2.7	2.5	2.4	2.04	68.5	8.0	6.8	6.4	6.0	5.6	4.92
51.0	3.5	3.0	2.8	2.6	2.5	2.1	69.0	8.2	7.0	6.6	6.1	5.7	4.92
51.5	3.6	3.1	2.9	2.7	2.5		69.5	8.3	7.1	6.7	6.2	5.8	
52.0	3.7	3.1	3.0	2.8	2.6	2.22	70.0	8.5	7.2	6.8	6.3	5.9	5.1
52.5	3.8	3.2	3.0	2.8	2.6		70.5	8.6	7.3	6.9	6.4	6.0	
53.0	3.9	3.3	3.1	2.9	2.7	2.34	71.0	8.7	7.4	7.0	6.5	6.1	5.22
53.5	4.0	3.4	3.2	3.0	2.8		71.5	8.9	7.5	7.1	6.6	6.2	
54.0	4.1	3.5	3.3	3.1	2.9	2.46	72.0	9.0	7.6	7.2	6.7	6.3	5.4
54.5	4.2	3.6	3.4	3.2	2.9		72.5	9.1	7.7	7.3	6.8	6.4	
55.0	4.3	3.7	3.5	3.2	3.0	2.58	73.0	9.2	7.8	7.4	6.9	6.4	5.52
55.5	4.4	3.8	3.5	3.3	3.1		73.5	9.4	8.0	7.5	7.0	6.5	
56.0	4.6	3.9	3.6	3.4	3.2	2.76	74.0	9.5	8.1	7.6	7.1	6.6	5.7
56.5	4.7	4.0	3.7	3.5	3.3		74.5	9.6	8.2	7.7	7.2	6.7	
57.0	4.8	4.1	3.8	3.6	3.4	2.88	75.0	9.7	8.2	7.8	7.3	6.8	5.82
57.5	4.9	4.2	3.9	3.7	3.4		75.5	9.8	8.3	7.9	7.4	6.9	
58.0	5.1	4.3	4.0	3.8	3.5	3.06	76.0	9.9	8.4	7.9	7.4	6.9	5.94
58.5	5.2	4.4	4.2	3.9	3.6		76.5	10.0	8.5	8.0	7.5	7.0	
59.0	5.3	4.5	4.3	4.0	3.7	3.18	77.0	10.1	8.6	8.1	7.6	7.1	6.06
59.5	5.5	4.6	4.4	4.1	3.8		77.5	10.2	8.7	8.2	7.7	7.2	
60.0	5.6	4.8	4.5	4.2	3.9	3.36	78.0	10.4	8.8	8.3	7.8	7.2	6.24
60.5	5.7	4.9	4.6	4.3	4.0		78.5	10.5	8.9	8.3	7.8	7.3	
61.0	5.9	5.0	4.7	4.4	4.1	3.54	79.0	10.6	9.0	8.4	7.9	7.4	6.36
61.5	6.0	5.1	4.8	4.5	4.2		79.5	10.7	9.1	8.5	8.0	7.5	
62.0	6.2	5.2	4.9	4.6	4.3	3.72	80.0	10.8	9.1	8.6	8.1	7.5	6.48
62.5	6.3	5.4	5.0	4.7	4.4		80.5	10.9	9.2	8.7	8.1	7.6	
63.0	6.5	5.5	5.2	4.8	4.5	3.9	81.0	11.0	9.3	8.8	8.2	7.7	6.6
63.5	6.6	5.6	5.3	5.0	4.6		81.5	11.1	9.4	8.8	8.3	7.7	
64.0	6.7	5.7	5.4	5.1	4.7	4.02	82.0	11.2	9.5	8.9	8.4	7.8	6.72
64.5	6.9	5.9	5.5	5.2	4.8		82.5	11.3	9.6	9.0	8.4	7.8	
65.0	7.0	6.0	5.6	5.3	4.9	4.2	83.0	11.4	9.6	9.1	8.5	7.9	6.84
65.5	7.2	6.1	5.7	5.4	5.0		83.5	11.5	9.7	9.2	8.6	8.0	
66.0	7.3	6.2	5.9	5.5	5.1	4.38	84.0	11.5	9.8	9.2	8.7	8.1	6.9
66.5	7.5	6.4	6.0	5.6	5.2		84.5	11.6	9.9	9.3	8.7	8.2	

WEIGHT FOR HEIGHT (Stature) FOR BOTH BOYS AND GIRLS

Height	Median	Percents of Median 85%	80%	75%	70%	60%	Height	Median	Percents of Median 85%	80%	75%	70%	60%
85.0cm	12.0kg	10.2kg	9.6kg	9.0kg	8.4kg	7.2 kg	107.5cm	17.7kg	15.0kg	14.1kg	13.3kg	12.4kg	10.68
85.5	12.1	10.3	9.7	9.1	8.5		108.0	17.8	15.2	14.3	13.4	12.5	
86.0	12.2	10.4	9.8	9.2	8.6	7.32	108.5	18.0	15.3	14.4	13.5	12.6	10.86
86.5	12.3	10.5	9.8	9.2	8.6		109.0	18.1	15.4	14.5	13.6	12.7	
87.0	12.4	10.6	9.9	9.3	8.7	7.44	109.5	18.3	15.5	14.6	13.7	12.8	
87.5	12.5	10.6	10.0	9.4	8.8		110.0	18.4	15.7	14.8	13.8	12.9	11.04
88.0	12.6	10.7	10.1	9.5	8.8	7.56	110.5	18.6	15.8	14.9	14.0	13.0	11.28
88.5	12.8	10.8	10.2	9.6	8.9		111.0	18.8	16.0	15.0	14.1	13.1	
89.0	12.9	10.9	10.3	9.7	9.0	7.74	111.5	18.9	16.1	15.1	14.2	13.3	
89.5	13.0	11.0	10.4	9.7	9.1		112.0	19.1	16.2	15.3	14.3	13.4	11.46
90.0	13.1	11.1	10.5	9.8	9.2	7.86	112.5	19.3	16.4	15.4	14.4	13.5	
90.5	13.2	11.2	10.6	9.9	9.2		113.0	19.4	16.5	15.5	14.6	13.6	11.64
91.0	13.3	11.3	10.7	10.0	9.3	7.98	113.5	19.6	16.7	15.7	14.7	13.7	
91.5	13.4	11.4	10.8	10.1	9.4		114.0	19.8	16.8	15.8	14.8	13.8	11.88
92.0	13.6	11.5	10.8	10.2	9.5	8.16	114.5	19.9	16.9	16.0	15.0	14.0	
92.5	13.7	11.6	10.9	10.3	9.6		115.0	20.1	17.1	16.1	15.1	14.1	12.06
93.0	13.8	11.7	11.0	10.4	9.7	8.28	115.5	20.3	17.3	16.2	15.2	14.2	
93.5	13.9	11.8	11.1	10.4	9.7		116.0	20.5	17.4	16.4	15.4	14.3	12.3
94.0	14.0	11.9	11.2	10.5	9.8	8.4	116.5	20.7	17.6	16.5	15.5	14.5	
94.5	14.2	12.0	11.3	10.6	9.9		117.0	20.8	17.7	16.7	15.6	14.6	12.48
95.0	14.3	12.1	11.4	10.7	10.0	8.58	117.5	21.0	17.9	16.8	15.8	14.7	
95.5	14.4	12.2	11.5	10.8	10.1		118.0	21.2	18.0	17.0	15.9	14.9	12.72
96.0	14.5	12.3	11.6	10.9	10.2	8.7	118.5	21.4	18.2	17.1	16.1	15.0	
96.5	14.7	12.5	11.7	11.0	10.3		119.0	21.6	18.4	17.3	16.2	15.1	12.96
97.0	14.8	12.6	11.8	11.1	10.3	8.88	119.5	21.8	18.5	17.4	16.4	15.3	
97.5	14.9	12.7	11.9	11.2	10.4		120.0	22.0	18.7	17.6	16.5	15.4	13.2
98.0	15.0	12.8	12.0	11.3	10.5	9.0	120.5	22.2	18.9	17.8	16.7	15.5	
98.5	15.2	12.9	12.1	11.4	10.6		121.0	22.4	19.1	17.9	16.8	15.7	13.44
99.0	15.3	13.0	12.2	11.5	10.7	9.18	121.5	22.6	19.2	18.1	17.0	15.8	
99.5	15.4	13.1	12.3	11.6	10.8		122.0	22.8	19.4	18.3	17.1	16.0	13.68
100.0	15.6	13.2	12.4	11.7	10.9	9.36	122.5	23.1	19.6	18.4	17.3	16.1	
100.5	15.7	13.3	12.6	11.8	11.0		123.0	23.3	19.8	18.6	17.5	16.3	
101.0	15.8	13.5	12.7	11.9	11.1	9.48	123.5	23.5	20.0	18.8	17.6	16.5	13.98
101.5	16.0	13.6	12.8	12.0	11.2		124.0	23.7	20.2	19.0	17.8	16.6	
102.0	16.1	13.7	12.9	12.1	11.3	9.66	124.5	24.0	20.4	19.2	18.0	16.8	14.22
102.5	16.2	13.8	13.0	12.2	11.4		125.0	24.2	20.6	19.4	18.2	16.9	14.52
103.0	16.4	13.9	13.1	12.3	11.5	9.84	125.5	24.4	20.8	19.6	18.3	17.1	
103.5	16.5	14.0	13.2	12.4	11.6		126.0	24.7	21.0	19.7	18.5	17.3	14.82
104.0	16.7	14.2	13.3	12.5	11.7		126.5	24.9	21.2	19.9	18.7	17.5	
104.5	16.8	14.3	13.4	12.6	11.8	10.02	127.0	25.2	21.4	20.1	18.9	17.6	15.12
105.0	16.9	14.4	13.6	12.7	11.9	10.14	127.5	25.4	21.6	20.4	19.1	17.8	
105.5	17.1	14.5	13.7	12.8	12.0		128.0	25.7	21.8	20.6	19.3	18.0	15.42
106.0	17.2	14.6	13.8	12.9	12.1	10.32	128.5	26.0	22.1	20.8	19.5	18.2	
106.5	17.4	14.8	13.9	13.0	12.2		129.0	26.2	22.3	21.0	19.7	18.4	15.72
107.0	17.5	14.9	14.0	13.1	12.3	10.5	129.5	26.5	22.5	21.2	19.9	18.6	
							130.0	26.8	22.8	21.4	20.1	18.7	16.08

Appendix 3
OXFAM FEEDING KITS AND EQUIPMENT

Introduction

The OXFAM Kits (OFK) supply both equipment and guidance for nutritional surveillance and feeding vulnerable and severely malnourished groups. The Kits are designed for refugee situations to allow a relief team to start work as soon as they arrive in the field, and may be adapted to other circumstances.

Background

Most of the equipment in the Kits could be bought locally in 'normal times', and the use of local resources is ideal when they are available and time is not short. However, in the past relief personnel have often spent valuable time searching for cups, bowls and cooking pots in refugee situations, and delays cannot be justified when Selective Feeding Procedures are urgently needed. Later, if the programme enlarges, personnel with local knowledge could provide invaluable assistance in locating more equipment, if it is available in the relief area.

These Kits do *not* contain food and are *not* designed to provide total feeding for the whole community. The use of the Kits presumes that the bulk of the community either has its own supplies or is benefiting from a general feeding programme.

OFK 1 - NUTRITION SURVEILLANCE EQUIPMENT

This includes items for screening and ongoing monitoring and can be used in conjunction with the Feeding Kits.

OFK 2 - SUPPLEMENTARY FEEDING KIT (250)

This is designed for the Supplementary Feeding of vulnerable groups e.g. children under five, and other members of the community whose nutritional state is particularly poor. The Kit caters for 250 people and, besides feeding and cooking equipment, includes items for simple screening and monitoring. The Kit can be used by members of the refugee community who have undergone some basic training.

Stoves and other sources of heat for cooking are not included as conditions vary from one situation to another. Fuel is often a major problem. Locally constructed mud stoves may help to conserve limited supplies of wood.

OFK 3 - THERAPEUTIC FEEDING KIT (100)

This is designed to cater for 100 severely malnourished children requiring Therapeutic Feeding (Nutritional Rehabilitation), but it is not envisaged that this Kit will be used as often as OFK No. 2 and No. 5 (Supplementary).

The Kit can be used by trained staff who are able to recognise and respond to the main health problems associated with severe malnutrition, e.g. diarrhoea, dehydration, infection etc.

Medical care is secondary to feeding but overall supervision needs to be by a suitably experienced person. Basic drugs and medical supplies are not included as they are normally available through the camp health service, government system, relief supplies etc.

OFK 4 - MINI SURVEY KIT

This was designed to enable relief workers, immediately on arrival in a given situation and using simple survey techniques, to measure the nutritional status of refugees and village communities. The Kit fits into a small rucksack.

OFK 5 - SUPPLEMENTARY FEEDING KIT (500)

This Kit is designed for the supplementary feeding of *500* children, and contains similar equipment to that in Kit No. 2 (the only difference being in quantity).

OXFAM NUTRITIONAL SURVEILLANCE EQUIPMENT OFK 1

For Nutritional Surveys and Ongoing Monitoring (Children)

1	Height Stick (150cm) and 2 'read off' markers - wooden
1	Length Board (100cm) - wooden
1	Standard 1 Kg Weight (to check scales)
1	Salter Spring Scales - 25Kg
1	Salter Spring Scales - 50Kg
10	Fibre Glass Tape Measures
2	Instruction Leaflets for Shakir Strips
2	Hardback Books (for Registers)
10	Exercise Books
2	pairs Scissors
10	Pens, 10 Pencils, 2 Rubbers, 2 Pencil Sharpeners
2	Rulers, 2 Clipboards, 1 box Drawing Pins
1	packet Graph Paper, 5 Indelible Ink Marker Pens
800	Identity Bracelets
10	Weight for Height Graph Sheets + 5 Weight/Height Tables
2	Weight/Height Wall Charts
1	Pocket Calculator & Batteries
1	Holdall - heavy duty nylon

BOOKS

2	'Oxfam's Practical Guide to Selective Feeding Programmes'
1	'Management of Nutritional Emergencies in Large Populations' by de Ville de Goyet et al. - WHO, Geneva
1	'Nutrition for Developing Countries' by Maurice King et al.- TALC, U.K.
1	'Control of Communicable Diseases' by Benenson (also available in French) - American Public Health Association
1	British National Formulary
1	'Oxfam's Practical Guide to Refugee Health Care' by Dr. Paul Shears

Packed in one Triwall container - 106cm x 37cm x 27cm

OXFAM SUPPLEMENTARY FEEDING KIT (BOX A)   OFK 2

Nutritional Surveillance Equipment (Children)

1	Height Stick (150cm) and 2 'read off' markers - wooden
1	Length Board (100cm) - wooden
1	Standard 1 Kg Weight (to check scales)
1	Salter Spring Scales - 25Kg
1	Salter Spring Scales - 50Kg
10	Fibre Glass Tape Measures
2	Instruction Leaflets for Shakir Strips
2	Hardback Books (for Registers)
10	Exercise Books
2	pairs Scissors
10	Pens, 10 Pencils, 2 Rubbers, 2 Pencil Sharpeners
2	Rulers, 2 Clipboards, 1 box Drawing Pins
1	packet Graph Paper, 5 Indelible Ink Marker Pens
800	Identity Bracelets
10	Weight for Height Graph Sheets + 5 Weight/Height Tables
2	Weight/Height Wall Charts
1	Pocket Calculator & Batteries
1	Holdall - heavy duty nylon

BOOKS

2	'Oxfam's Practical Guide to Selective Feeding Programmes'
1	'Management of Nutritional Emergencies in Large Populations' by de Ville de Goyet et al. - WHO, Geneva
1	'Nutrition for Developing Countries' by Maurice King et al.- TALC, U.K.
1	'Control of Communicable Diseases' by Benenson (also available in French) - American Public Health Association
1	British National Formulary
1	'Oxfam's Practical Guide to Refugee Health Care' by Dr. Paul Shears

Packed in one Triwall container - 106cm x 37cm x 27cm

OXFAM SUPPLEMENTARY FEEDING KIT (BOX B)   OFK 2

Feeding Equipment to cater for 250 Adults and Children

1	Cooking Pot (100 litres) with Lid
1	Cooking Pot (50 litres) with Lid
2	Wooden Paddles for stirring food
300	Cups (plastic)
300	Bowls (plastic)
100	Plastic Teaspoons
6	Metal Spoons
2	Scoops
2	Measuring Jugs
2	Ladles
2	Metal Whisks
2	Tin Openers
1	Scrubbing Brush
4	Buckets with Lids
2	Large Jerry Cans
500	Water Sterilising Tablets (Novo Tabs)

BOOKS

2	'Oxfam's Practical Guide to Selective Feeding Programmes'
1	'Guidelines for Training Community Health Workers in Nutrition' - WHO, Geneva
1	'Medical Care in Developing Countries' by Maurice King
1	'Oxfam's Practical Guide to Refugee Health Care' by Dr. Paul Shears

Packed in one Triwall container 105cm x 73cm x 63cm

OXFAM THERAPEUTIC FEEDING KIT (BOX A) OFK 3

Weighing and Measuring Equipment to cater for 100 severely malnourished children

1	Height Stick (150cm) and 2 'read off' markers - wooden
1	Length Board (100cm) - wooden
1	Standard 1 Kg Weight (to check scales)
1	Salter Spring Scales - 25Kg
1	Salter Spring Scales - 50Kg
10	Fibre Glass Tape Measures
2	Instruction Leaflets for Shakir Strips
1	Hardback Book (for Register)
1	packet Graph Paper
5	Exercise Books, 5 Pens, 5 Pencils
1	Ruler, 1 Pencil Sharpener, 5 Indelible Ink Marker Pens
1	Clipboard
1	pair Scissors
500	Plastic Identity Bracelets
500	Medical Record Cards
600	Milk Cards
1	Plastic Storage Box
1	Weight for Height Wall Chart
1	Pocket Calculator & Batteries
2	Weight/Height Tables

BOOKS

1	'Management of Nutritional Emergencies in Large Populations' by de Ville de Goyet et al. - WHO, Geneva
2	'Oxfam's Practical Guide to Selective Feeding Programmes'
1	Paediatric Vade Mecum
1	British National Formulary
1	'Oxfam's Practical Guide to Refugee Health Care' by Dr. Paul Shears.

Packed in one Triwall container - 106cm x 37cm x 27cm

OXFAM THERAPEUTIC FEEDING KIT (BOX B)   OFK 3

Feeding Equipment to cater for 100 severely malnourished children

2	Cooking Pots (50 litres) with Lids
2	Wooden Paddles for stirring food
120	Cups
120	Bowls
50	Metal Teaspoons
250	Plastic Teaspoons
2	Measuring Jugs (2 litres)
2	Scoops
2	Ladles
2	Whisks
2	Tin Openers
1	Food Scale
1	Alarm Clock
1	Scrubbing Brush
2	Large Plastic Jerry Cans
4	Buckets with Lids
2	Hurricane Lamps
12	Candles (Nightlights) and Matches
1	Torch and 4 Batteries
500	Water Purifying Tablets
50	Nasogastric Tubes, Syringes × 5, sticky tape (assorted sizes)

Packed in one Triwall container 105cm × 73cm × 63cm

OXFAM 'MINI' SURVEY KIT   OFK 4

- 1   25Kg Hanging Scale and Pants
- 10   Fibre Glass Tape Measures
- 2   Exercise Books
- 1   Clipboard
- 10   Weight for Height Graph Sheet + Weight/Height Tables
- 1   pack of Graph Paper
- 2   Pens
- 2   Pencils
- 2   Rulers
- 1   Pencil Sharpener
- 1   Rubber
- 1   box Drawing Pins
- 2   'Oxfam's Practical Guide to Selective Feeding Programmes'
- 1   'Management of Nutritional Emergencies in Large Populations' by de Ville de Goyet et al. - WHO, Geneva
- 1   'Oxfam's Practical Guide to Refugee Health Care' by Dr Paul Shears
- 1   Weight/Height Wall Chart
- 1   Pocket Calculator & Batteries
- 1   Rucksack

SUPPLEMENTARY FEEDING KIT FOR 500 CHILDREN   OFK 5

The contents are identical to those of OFK 2 with the inclusion of an extra Box B, to enable catering for up to 500 children.

Appendix 4

APPROXIMATE KILOCALORIE/PROTEIN VALUES FOR SOME USEFUL RELIEF AND INDIGENOUS FOODS

Type	Food	Kcalories (per 100gm)	Protein/gm
Fats	Vegetable Oil	900Kcal.	–
	Butter	750 "	–
Sugars	Sugar	400Kcal.	–
	Honey	250 "	–
Cereals	Maize		10.0
	Rice		7.0
	Sorghum	350Kcal.	10.0
	Wheat		11.0
Vegetables	Groundnuts		20.0
	Chickpeas		20.0
	Lentils	350Kcal.	20.0
	Soyabeans		35.0
Meat/eggs	Pork	500Kcal.	10.0
	Beef	250 "	16.0
	Goat	150 "	16.0
	Fish(dry)	300 "	63.0
	Eggs	150 "	13.0
Relief Foods	CSM	380Kcal.	18.3
	DSM	356 "	30.0
	Humana	439 "	23.1
	Curate Protein Tonic	240 "	90.0
	Soy-Wheat-fortified	350 "	12-14.0

ENERGY REQUIREMENTS

Recommended daily energy requirements measured in Kcal.

Moderately active adult	Male	3000
	Female	2200
Sedentary adult	Male	2500
	Female	2000
Pregnant woman		2500
Lactating woman		2500
Child - up to 5 years	Male	1200 - 1900
	Female	1200 - 1800
Child - over 5 years	Male	2000 - 3000
	Female	1900 - 2200

Survival energy requirements in Kcal.

		Emergency Subsistence	Temporary Maintenance
0 - 2 years		1000	1000
3 - 5 years		1250	1500
6 - 9 years		1500	1750
10 - 17 years		2000	2500
Pregnant or lactating woman		2000	2500
Normal (sedentary)	Male	1900	2200
	Female	1600	1800
Moderate labour		2000	2500
Heavy labour		2500	3000
Very heavy labour		3000	3500

PROTEIN REQUIREMENTS

Recommended daily protein requirements

Adult (sedentary)	35gm
Baby	3gm/kg
Child 6 months - 4 years	35gm
Pregnant woman	65gm
Lactating woman	65gm

Ideally 10-15% of the protein should be of animal origin.

Appendix 5

RECIPES

General Points:

Indigenous Foods: The use of suitable indigenous foods and local recipes should be encouraged for Supplementary Feeding diets. Where such food is not available, a relief food should be provided which is as similar as possible to the indigenous food and therefore readily acceptable to those attending the Programme. This is essential in a SFP since if the people do not like the food they will not attend for feeding.

Pre-cooked Foods: Some supplementary relief foods are pre-cooked and only need to be reconstituted with water (hot or cold) before being served. These foods are convenient when large numbers of people are to be fed as the preparation procedure is a very simple one. Supplementary foods are generally more acceptable if served hot, even if not actually cooked.

Sugar: Sugar (i.e. extra Kcals.) can be added to supplementary foods when it is available, although some already have sugar in the premix.

Oil: A liquid vegetable oil is much easier to deal with than the semi-solid butter oil. When butter oil is the only type available it should be melted before being added to any of the supplementary 'porridge' type foods. It is also necessary to melt the oil before mixing the HEM Premix. The oil can only be distributed evenly throughout the whole mixture if it is in liquid form.

Water: Any water being used in the preparation of Supplementary or Therapeutic diets must be treated by boiling or with sterilising tablets, unless known to be pure and uncontaminated or from a 'safe' source.

Where water has to be drawn straight from a muddy river or stream, it should be left to stand in suitable containers (e.g. oil drums) for several hours to allow sedimentation to occur. This process can be speeded up by sprinkling a few grains of DSM or sand on the surface of the water. When clear, the top half of the water can be decanted and treated before use. Where possible water should be left standing in the sunlight as this alone will kill many harmful bacteria and organisms. Filtration will be of use in clearing the water of amoebae, cysts, etc. Advice on these procedures is available in the Oxfam Field Directors' Handbook.

Calculated amounts of ingredients for Basic Mixes — using edible portions of raw foods

Staples (g) / Supplement (g)		Oats	Wheat	Rice	Sorghum, millet	Maize	Potato	Sweet Potato	Yam	Taro, Cocoyam	Banana	Plantain	Cassava Flour, gari
Legume	(g)	75 / 5	80 / 10	65 / 25	75 / 10	55 / 35	320 / 20	125 / 50	165 / 40	150 / 45	105 / 55	85 / 55	40 / 55
Soybeans	(g)	60 / 10	60 / 15	55 / 20	55 / 15	50 / 25	250 / 20	150 / 25	175 / 20	150 / 20	140 / 25	115 / 30	50 / 30
Dried skimmed milk	(g)	65 / 5	65 / 10	65 / 15	60 / 15	60 / 15	280 / 15	175 / 20	190 / 15	180 / 15	165 / 20	150 / 20	60 / 20
Dried whole milk	(g)	55 / 10	55 / 15	45 / 25	45 / 20	40 / 25	220 / 20	100 / 30	115 / 30	115 / 25	100 / 30	90 / 30	35 / 30
Chick or lean meat	(g)	65 / 10	65 / 20	65 / 25	65 / 25	65 / 35	300 / 25	180 / 35	210 / 35	195 / 30	185 / 40	160 / 45	70 / 45
Fresh fish	(g)	65 / 15	70 / 30	70 / 30	70 / 25	70 / 20	310 / 25	210 / 35	240 / 35	220 / 40	210 / 40	180 / 45	75 / 50
Egg	(g)	65 / 10	65 / 25	65 / 30	60 / 30	65 / 25	300 / 25	180 / 35	220 / 25	190 / 25	190 / 30	150 / 45	60 / 50

See notes 1-6 on P.83.

Extract from 'Manual on Feeding Infants and Young Children' by Cameron and Hofvander. Reprinted by kind permission of the Oxford University Press.

NOTES

1. The least amount of protein food is used to supplement the staple to provide the basis of a meal for a child of about 2 years old.
2. To each of these basic mixes 10gm of oil, OR 5gm of oil and 10gm of sugar, OR 20gm of sugar should be added.
3. Each mix then provides about 350Kcal (approximately one-third of the daily needs of a 2 year old child).
4. Each mix has the same protein value and provides the approximate equivalent of 5-6gm of reference protein.
5. The weights given for the staple and the supplement are for raw foods.
6. The volumes of most of the basic mixes are between 200-300ml when the water absorbed by the food is taken into account.

RECIPES FOR SUPPLEMENTARY AND THERAPEUTIC FEEDING

NOTE: 1 litre water = 1kg
1 litre oil = 0.9kg
1 litre HEM Premix = 1kg

1. UGANDA SUPPLEMENTARY PORRIDGE MIX

This recipe can also be used with other cereals and milks - e.g. Bulgar wheat and CSM - although small adjustments in quantities may be necessary to get the right consistency, and calories will have to be re-calculated.

This particular mix gives 1.25Kcals per ml (1Kcal/ml without the sugar); therefore, 1 full Oxfam cup (400ml) = 500 Kcals.

A premix is made mixing posho (maize flour), dried skimmed milk (DSM) and sugar and then thoroughly mixing in oil.

Premix quantities per feed

No.of children	OIL/litres	DSM/kg	POSHO/kg	SUGAR/kg
10	200ml	250gm	500gm	125gm
20	400ml	500gm	1kg	250gm
30	600ml	750gm	1.5kg	375gm
40	800ml	1kg	2kg	500gm
50	1 litre	1.25kg	2.5kg	625gm
100	2 litres	2.50kg	5kg	1.25kg
200	4 litres	5kg	10kg	2.50kg

To make the porridge

For 20 children mix 2.10kg premix in 6L of water
For 50 children mix 5.25kg premix in 15L of water
For 100 children mix 10.5kg premix in 30L of water
For 150 children mix 15.75kg premix in 45L of water
For 200 children mix 21kg   premix in 60L of water (total volume = approx. 80L)

Add some of the boiled water to the mixture to make a paste and get out the lumps, then add it to the rest of the boiled water and cook for about 30 minutes.

The porridge should be thick, but liquid enough to be drunk from a cup.

Quantities of dry ingredients required per week

No.of children	OIL/litres	DSM/kg	POSHO/kg	SUGAR/kg
10	2.8	3.5	7	1.75
20	5.6	7	14	3.5
30	8.4	10.5	21	5.25
40	11.2	14	28	7
50	14	17.5	35	8.75
100	28	35	70	17.5
200	56	70	140	35
400	112	140	280	70

MIXTURES:

Mixtures of food items are presented by volumetric proportions. In addition volumetric and weight quantities are calculated for various numbers of people. Dried supplies should be mixed with oil before adding water (where appropriate), while mixing thoroughly.

2. DRIED SKIM MILK (DSM) AND SUGAR MIXTURE

A 400ml portion contains 165 Kilocalories and 15 grams of protein.

Basic formula by volumes: 5 parts DSM
                          20 parts water
                           1 part sugar

Examples:	**100 servings**	**225 servings**
DSM	8.5 litres (4.25kg)	19 litres (9.5kg)
Water	34 litres	76 litres
Sugar	1.75 litres (1.75kg)	4 litres (4kg)
Total fluid volume:	40 litres fluid	90 litres fluid (approx.)

This mixture alone is not normally adequate for Supplementary Feeding Programme diets; recipes 1 or 3 would be more suitable. DSM by itself can be made up 1 part DSM to 6 parts water; it mixes quite well with cold water, but a whisk makes the job easier.

3. DRIED SKIM MILK (DSM) OIL AND SUGAR MIXTURE

A 400ml portion contains 250 Kilocalories and 14 grams of protein.

Basic formula by volumes: 5 parts DSM
20 parts water
1 part sugar
$\frac{1}{2}$ oil

Examples:	100 servings	240 servings
DSM	8 litres (4kg)	20 litres (10kg)
Water	33 litres	80 litres
Sugar	1.6 litres (1.6kg)	4 litres (4kg)
Oil	800ml (800gm)	2 litres (2kg)
Total fluid volume:	40 litres (approx.)	96 litres (approx.)

4. CORN-SOYA MILK (CSM) OIL AND SUGAR MIXTURE

A 300ml portion contains 270 Kilocalories and 11 grams of protein.

Basic formula by volumes: 10 parts CSM
20 parts water
1 part sugar
1 part oil

(If oil and sugar are not available, CSM by itself can be made up 1 part CSM to 2-3 parts water.)

Examples:	100 servings	200 servings	315 servings
CSM	11 litres (5.5kg)	22 litres (11kg)	35 litres(17.5kg)
Water	22 litres	44 litres	70 litres
Sugar	1 litre (1kg)	2.25 litres (2.25kg)	3.5 litres (3.5kg)
Oil	1 litre (1kg)	2.25 litres (2.25kg)	3.5 litres (3.5kg)
Total fluid volume:	30 litres(approx.)	60 litres(approx.)	95 litres(approx.)

5. INSTANT CORN SOYA MILK (ICSM) (Precooked)

Basic formula by volumes: 1 part ICSM
1 part water (hot or cold)

If hot water is used the porridge will swell slightly, so extra water may be added. ICSM is sweetened but, like CSM, it will take added sugar and oil if required.

6. WHEAT SOYA BLEND (WSB)

Basic formula by volumes: 1 part WSB
                                           10 parts water

Mix the WSB to a smooth paste with a small quantity of water, add the rest of the water, bring to the boil and cook for 5 minutes.

Sugar should be added to the mixture before serving to children.

7. POST KWASHIORKOR FORTIFIED MIX (PKFM) (Precooked)

Basic formula by volumes: 1 part PKFM
                                           2 parts water (hot or cold)

PKFM will swell if mixed with hot water. It is a pre-sweetened, vanilla-flavoured mixture.

8. K-MIX-II

K-Mix-II is a UNICEF product used extensively in the treatment of severe malnutrition. It is very expensive and should only be used for the most severe cases. It is made up of:

    Calcium caseinate   3 parts by weight
    Dried skimmed milk   5 parts by weight
    Sucrose   10 parts by weight

K-Mix-II powder has to be mixed with a liquid vegetable oil and water in the following proportions:

    K-Mix-II 100gm
    Oil   60gm
    Water   1 litre

Mix the K-Mix-II and the oil together thoroughly and then add the water slowly, stirring well.

The reconstituted milk should be served immediately or the oil tends to separate out. The volume of feed given to each child is calculated according to the weight of the child.

9. HIGH ENERGY MILK (HEM)

The recipe given here was devised and used by the MRC in Uganda and in the Oxfam TFC in Wollo, Ethiopia in 1973/74. It can be mixed centrally and distributed to the Feeding Centres, or can be mixed from the raw ingredients at each Centre.

HEM is made in two stages: i. The premix
                                    ii. The liquid milk

The premix has a shelf life of at least a week and much longer if storage facilities are ideal; it can be stored in suitable clean, covered containers (e.g. oil drums) or in large, strong plastic bags.

The premix is made in the following proportions:

DSM 420gm
Sugar 250gm
Oil 320gm

The premix is usually mixed in larger quantities and stored. A 40kg batch can be made (and stored as above) in the following proportions:

DSM 34 litres (17kg)   )
Sugar 10.7 litres (10.2kg)) = 40kg premix
Oil   14 litres (12.8kg))

Method: Mix DSM and sugar and then add the oil. Mix thoroughly.

Ideally Electrolytes can be added to this mixture in the following proportions:

Potassium chloride   5.2gm)
) per kg of premix
Magnesium hydroxide 2.4gm)

Before reconstituting this premix with water to make the HEM, it is necessary to stir the mixture thoroughly to ensure that the oil is evenly distributed (a large wooden paddle is provided in the Oxfam Feeding Kit for this purpose). After standing for a few hours the oil is inclined to separate out and settle at the bottom of the container.

1 litre of premix conveniently weighs 1kg, but weighing scales should be used when possible as this is more accurate than the volumetric measurement.

The HEM premix should be reconstituted in the following proportions:

PREMIX kg/litres	WATER/litres	FINAL VOLUME/litres
0.18 +	0.815 =	1
0.95	4.05	5
1.85	8.15	10
2.80	12.22	15
3.70	16.30	20
4.60	20.37	25
5.55	24.44	30
6.45	28.52	35
7.40	32.60	40
8.30	36.66	45
9.25	40.70	50

By calculating the average weight of the children it is possible to work out the approximate volume of HEM required at each feed. Usually an average of 250-300ml per child, i.e. 25 litres of HEM will feed about 80-100 children.

The HEM should be reconstituted immediately before the feed to prevent the oil separating out. It is more acceptable to the children if served hot.

The volume required for each child should be calculated according to the weight of the child. (See Chapter 7, 7.2.1.)

NOTE: If no weighing scales are available use the following simplified method for making an adequate High Energy Milk:

DSM 6 parts
Oil   2 parts
Sugar 1 part

Dilute with 4 parts of water = 100Kcals + 4gm Protein in 100ml HEM.

HEM quantities required

Using as an average a child weighing 9kg, consuming 1.35 litres of HEM (approx. 1350Kcals) per day:

	child/day	Kcals
DSM	111.7gm	395
Sugar	66.5gm	264
Oil	83.8gm	747

No. of children	Weekly			Monthly		
	DSM/kg	OIL/litre	SUGAR/kg	DSM/kg	OIL/litre	SUGAR/kg
40	31.3	23.46	18.6	134.1	100.5	79
50	39.6	29.3	23.2	167.6	125	99.7
60	46.9	35.19	27.9	201	150.8	119.7
70	54.7	41	32.5	234.4	175.3	139.6
80	62.5	46.9	37.2	267.8	201	159.6
90	70.3	52.79	41.8	301.3	226	179.5
100	78.1	54.6	46.5	335.1	249	199.5

10. FULL CREAM POWDERED MILK

NOTE: The priority must always be to re-establish breast-feeding (see text).

For babies up to 3 months old

Milk powder:	1 level teaspoonful
Boiled water:	30ml
Sugar:	1 level teaspoonful *per feed*
Daily requirement:	150ml of the mixture per kg body weight per 24 hours
Volume per feed:	One-fifth of daily total at each of five feeds at four-hourly intervals

For babies over 3 months old

Milk powder:	1 rounded teaspoonful
Boiled water:	30ml
Sugar:	1 level teaspoonful *per feed*
Daily requirement:	150ml of the mixture per kg body weight per 24 hours
Volume per feed:	One-fifth of daily total at each of five feeds at four-hourly intervals

The parent/attendant should be shown how to measure out the liquid into a cup, the exact amount of milk powder plus 1 level teaspoonful of sugar, and how to mix them together for each feed.

The demonstration should be followed by the parent/attendant carrying out the instructions under supervision. Care must be taken with -

- preparing the feeding utensils: cup and spoon
- measuring the powders: the mixture must not be too concentrated
- ensuring that feeding bottles are *never* used

11. DRIED SKIM MILK (DSM) feed for infants up to 3 months old

NOTE: Only to be used in emergencies.

Ingredients for 1 litre

DSM	50gm
Sugar	50gm
*Cereal flour	30gm
Vegetable oil	30gm
Citric acid (fruit juice)	5gm
Water	900ml

* (any type, but flour from root crops - e.g. cassava - is *not* suitable)

Measure all ingredients with care. Mix all dry ingredients and add water gradually; bring slowly to boil and stir until flour is thoroughly cooked. Stir in the oil, then the citric acid.

For additional recipes see 'The Management of Nutritional Emergencies in Large Populations' - WHO, Geneva.

Appendix 6

Directions for the construction of a length board, height stick & height arch.

i. **Length board**

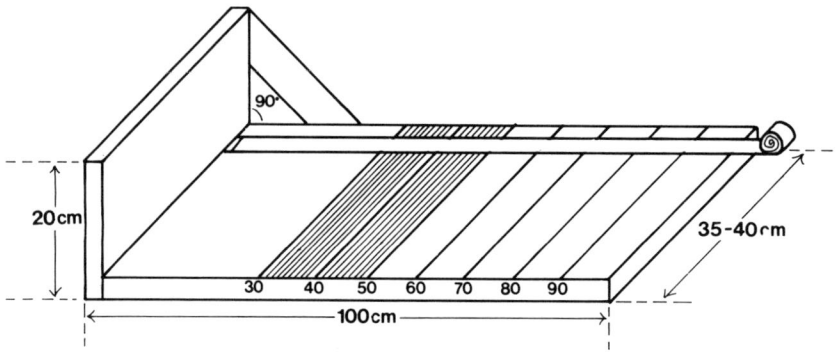

Supporting arm on **one** side to hold head board at right angles to base

1. Draw thick parallel lines at 10cm intervals from 30cm to end of board
2. Draw lighter lines at 1cm intervals across the board
3. Attach a tape measure down one side of the board
4. The wood used must be smooth and reasonably well-finished, to avoid problems with splinters and rough edges
5. It is necessary to construct a small measuring-block to ensure that the reading is taken at right angles

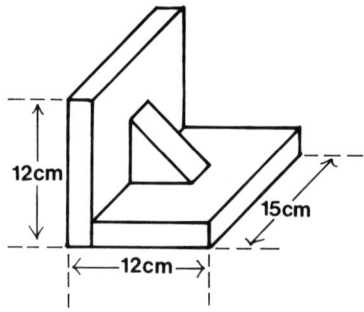

The same device can be used to accompany the height stick

ii. **Height stick**

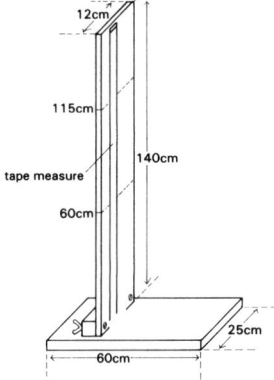

Two butterfly-wing bolts tightly fastened.

Supporting block firmly fastened to base block.

1. When assembled, ensure that the upright measuring stick is at right angles to the base and **very** firm.
2. Attach the tape measure down one side of the height board. It is useful to draw horizontal lines at 115cm and 60cm to assist with lining up.
3. Construct a small measuring block as for length board - but it only needs to be 12cm across instead of 15cm.

iii. **Height arch**

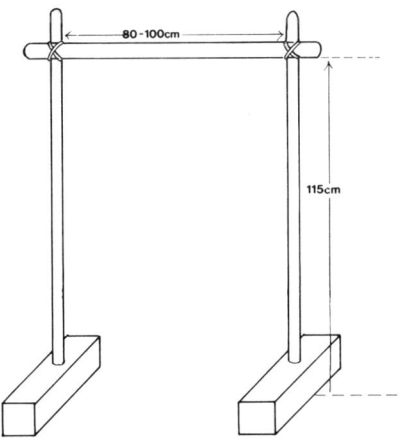

Blocks optional: sticks can be pushed into the ground and measured off. The cross-bar needs to be exactly 115cm high from ground level.

Appendix 7
FURTHER READING

1. Oxfam's Practical Guide to Refugee Health Care. Oxfam Working Paper No.2 - Oxfam Health Unit.
2. UNHCR Handbook for Emergencies - UNHCR, Geneva.
3. Refugee Community Health Care edited by S. Simmonds et al.- Oxford University Press.
4. Guidelines for Health Care in Refugee Camps: Refugee Health Unit, Somali Ministry of Health. Available through Oxfam.
5. Guidelines for Training Community Health Workers in Nutrition - WHO Offset Publication No.59.
6. The Management of Nutritional Emergencies in Large Populations: C. de Ville de Goyet et al - WHO, Geneva.
7. Measuring Change in Nutritional Status - WHO, Geneva 1983.
8. Manual on Feeding Infants and Young Children: Cameron and Hofvander - Oxford University Press.
9. Survival Strategies for and by Camp Refugees: Hanne Christensen - UN Research Institute for Social Development, Geneva.
10. Control of Communicable Diseases in Man: Abram Benenson - American Public Health Association.
11. Small Water Supplies: Ross Bulletin No.10: Cairncross and Feachem - London School of Hygiene and Tropical Medicine.
12. Small Excreta Disposal Systems: Ross Bulletin No.8: Cairncross and Feachem - London School of Hygiene and Tropical Medicine.